RESEARCH GUIDE FOR

CHINA'S RESPONSE

TO THE WEST

Prepared in cooperation with
the International Secretariat of
the Institute of Pacific Relations

Ssu-yü Teng

John K. Fairbank

with the collaboration of
E-tu Zen Sun
Chaoying Fang
and others

RESEARCH GUIDE FOR

CHINA'S RESPONSE

TO THE WEST

a documentary survey

1839–1923

Harvard
University
Press
Cambridge
1959

FOREWORD

This volume is designed to aid specialists in Chinese studies who seek to pursue those painstaking monographic and textual researches which alone can give the Western world a firmer grasp of modern China's history. While highly rewarding, such studies are not easy; and the Western specialist, who faces a translation problem more difficult than that of historians in China and Japan, needs to take full advantage of previous work in Western languages. Much of this work, in Western periodical literature, has been unavailable to (or at least unnoticed by) the recent compilers of source material collections on the Chinese mainland. On the other hand, some of the most useful studies of the persons, ideas, and events touched upon in *China's Response to the West* will be found in the Chinese periodical literature of an earlier day. At the same time, many sources which we quote remain as yet unstudied by any modern scholar, east or west.

In the first section of this volume, lists of Sources for further research and of Notes referring to the texts in *China's Response to the West* are given chapter by chapter in the same sequence as in the Table of Contents of that volume. Full citations of publications, including Chinese characters, are reserved for the Bibliography below. Characters for additional Chinese names and terms are given in the Glossary.

S. Y. T.

J. K. F.

September 1953

CONTENTS

NOTES AND SOURCES   1

BIBLIOGRAPHY   29

GLOSSARY   75

NOTES AND SOURCES

CORRECTIONS FOR CHINA'S RESPONSE TO THE WEST

On page 80, par. 4, for Ch. XV read Ch. XVI

On page 134, par. 2, for Ch. Xa read Ch. XIa

par. 3, for Ch. IIa read Ch. IIb

On page 148, par. 3, for Ch. XVI read Ch. XVIII

On page 149, par. 4, for [Yen Fu was] educated in the University of

Edinburgh read educated at the Greenwich

Naval Academy

On page 150, par. 2, for director of the Foochow Shipyard read teacher

at the Machiang Naval Academy at Foochow

On page 161, for DEMOCRACY read DEMOCRACY 18

On page 192, for (July 28, 1900) 5 read (July 28, 1900) 6

On page 212, par. 4, for obtaining the chü-jen read failing to obtain

the chü-jen

On page 215, par. 4, for chin-shih degree read higher degree;

for governorship read magistracy

On page 239, par. 3, for (1880-1939) read (1879 or 1880-1942)

NOTES AND SOURCES

Abbreviations Used in the Notes

CSK — *Ch'ing-shih kao* (Draft history of the Ch'ing Dynasty)

CSL — *Ch'ing shih-lu* (Veritable records of the Ch'ing Dynasty)

Hummel — Arthur W. Hummel (ed.), *Eminent Chinese of the Ch'ing Period (1644–1912)*, The Library of Congress, Washington, D. C., 1943–1944, 2 vols.

CSLC — *Ch'ing-shih lieh-chuan* (Historical biographies of the Ch'ing Dynasty)

CSPSR — *Chinese Social and Political Science Review*, Peking.

IWSM — *Ch'ou-pan i-wu shih-mo* (A complete account of the management of barbarian affairs):

                   TK — Tao-kuang period (1836–1850)

                   HF — Hsien-feng period (1851–1861)

                   TC — T'ung-chih period (1862–1874)

CHAPTER II. SOME ELEMENTS IN THE CHINESE INTELLECTUAL TRADITION

Sources

a. *Early Ch'ing "Nationalist" Thinkers*

The main source materials on the early Ch'ing thinkers are their own writings, some of which are mentioned in the text. On Huang Tsung-hsi (Huang Li-chou), *Li-chou i-chu hui-k'an*, which includes his chronological biography, is an important source. Professor Theodore de Bary of Columbia University is making a special study of Huang's *Ming-i tai-fang lu*. Hsieh Kuo-chen in his *Huang Li-chou hsueh-p'u* has collected extracts from Huang's writings in a scholarly account. A number of short articles on Huang's political philosophy have been produced in recent years, with various interpretations, but we forbear to list them in this introductory section.

Jih-chih-lu chi-shih is an edition of Ku Yen-wu's book with commentaries collected by Huang Ju-ch'eng, forming a work of encyclopaedic nature which is not included in Ku's collected writings, *T'ing-lin hsien-sheng i-shu hui-chi*. Among later studies on Ku, Hsieh Kuo-chen, *Ku Ning-jen hsueh-p'u*, and Ho I-k'un, *T'ing-lin hsueh-shu shu-p'ing*, should be noted.

The important source on Wang Fu-chih is undoubtedly *Wang Ch'uan-shan i-shu*. Two works on Wang's scholarship entitled *Ch'uan-shan hsueh-p'u*, one by Wang Yung-hsiang, including a *nien-p'u*, and the other by Chang Hsi-t'ang, are useful for reference. On Chu Chih-yü, *Shun-shui i-shu*, Liang Ch'i-ch'ao's sketch, and Matsumoto Sumio's *Mito gaku no genryū* are indispensable.

For general accounts of the early Ch'ing thinkers, see Liang Ch'i-ch'ao, *Chung-kuo chin-san-pai-nien hsueh-shu shih*; the same title by Ch'ien Mu; Hsiao Kung-ch'üan, *Chung-kuo cheng-chih ssu-hsiang shih*; and Liang's *Ch'ing-tai hsueh-shu kai-lun*. In English, see Lin Mou-sheng's *Men and Ideas, an Informal History of Chinese Political Thought*, and L. K. Tao, "A Chinese Political Theorist [Huang Tsung-hsi] of the Seventeenth Century." The little book by Ojima Sukema, *Chūgoku no kakumei shisō*, explores the important field of Chinese traditional political thought as related to modern revolutionary leaders, and in this connection touches upon Huang Tsung-hsi. Other Chinese studies include those of Hsiao I-shan in his *Ch'ing-tai t'ung-shih*; Kao Liang-tso, "Chung-kuo min-tsu ssu-hsiang chih hsien-tao che;" and Lo Er-kang, "Ming-wang hou Han-tsu ti tzu-chueh ho mi-mi chieh-she." On the secret societies, see also under reference note 13 below. For recent Western appraisals of Huang and other early Ch'ing philosophers see A. F. Wright, ed., *Studies in Chinese Thought* (memoir no. 75, the *American Anthropologist*, 55.5, part 2, Dec. 1953, 317 pp.), especially the chapter by David S. Nivison.

b. *The Early Jesuit Influence in China*

On the early Jesuit contact, see the works of K. S. Latourette, Arnold H. Rowbotham, Henri Bernard and Louis Pfister under their names in our Bibliography. For a brief historical survey of Nestorianism, Catholicism, and Protestantism in China, see K. S. Latourette, *A History of Christian Missions in China*; Hiyane Antei, *Shina Kirisuto-kyō shi*;

and Ishida Mikinosuke, "Shina bunka to Seihō bunka to no kōryū" (in *Iwanami kōza Tōyō shichō*). The best Japanese source on Christianity in the Ch'ing is probably Saeki Yoshirō, *Shinchō Kirisuto-kyō no kenkyū*. Yazawa Toshihiko, *Chūgoku to Seiyō bunka*, deals wholly with Catholicism in China, including the policies of K'ang-hsi and Yung-cheng toward papal missions. In Chinese, Yang Kuang-hsien, *Pu-te-i*, and Hsü Ch'ang-chih, *Sheng-ch'ao p'o-hsieh-chi*, are primary sources. The most thorough Western account of the Rites Controversy, as seen in its historical context and from the basic texts, is by Antonio S. Rosso, O.F.M., *Apostolic Legations to China*, which surveys the Roman Catholic approach down to the Ch'ien-lung period, with 185 pages of key documents. See also E. H. Pritchard's review of this work in *Far Eastern Quarterly*, 11.2: 241–244 (February 1952). Hsü Tsung-tse, *Ming-Ch'ing chien Yeh-su-hui-shih i-chu t'i-yao*, is an informative and useful source relating to works written or translated by Jesuits in China in the seventeenth and eighteenth centuries. Farther Bernard's list, "Les adaptations chinoises d'ouvrages européens," contains some 555 works for the period to 1688 alone. An earlier listing of such works is in Otake Fumio, "Mimmatsu irai seisho-kō," which includes items of the late-Ch'ing period. The articles of Ch'en Shou-yi and Chang Yin-lin (see in Bibliography below) contain much useful information and many ideas. See for example in *T'ien-hsia Monthly*, Ch'en Shou-yi's article, "The Religious Influence of Early Jesuits on Emperor Ch'ung-cheng of the Ming Dynasty." Yao Pao-yü, "Chi-tu-chiao chiao-shih shu-ju Hsi-yang wen-hua k'ao," is a well-documented study of the introduction into China of (a) Western astronomy and the calendar, (b) mathematics, (c) arms and military methods and (d) geography and maps. Yang Wei-yü and P'an Kung-chao, "K'ang-hsi-ti yü Hsi-yang wen-hua" (Emperor K'ang-hsi and Western culture), is an interesting short article. Chang En-lung, "Ming-Ch'ing liang-tai lai-Hua wai-jen k'ao-lueh," is a collection of more than three hundred short biographies of Europeans in China in the late Ming and early Ch'ing periods with identifications of their Chinese names, apparently based on Pfister. For articles containing much interesting material on the arguments used against the Jesuits and their science, see Chang Wei-hua, "Ming-Ch'ing chien Chung-Hsi ssu-hsiang chih ch'ung-t'u yü ying-hsiang," and "Ming Ch'ing chien Fo-Yeh chih cheng-pien"; Ch'en Teng-yuan, "Hsi-hsueh lai-Hua shih kuo-jen chih wu-tuan t'ai-tu"; and Ch'üan Han-sheng, "Ch'ing-mo ti Hsi-hsueh yuan-ch'u Chung-kuo shuo." Fang Hao, *Chung-kuo T'ien-chu-chiao-shih lun-ts'ung*, consists of essays on the Catholic influence in China, written by a Catholic scholar. Fang's "Ming-mo Hsi-yang huo-ch'i liu-ju wo-kuo chih shih-liao" concerns the role of the Jesuits regarding firearms. Many of these essays are reproduced in *Fang Hao wen-lu*. Cheng Shih-hsü, "Ming-Ch'ing liang-tai ti chün-chi pien-ko chi-ch'i ying-hsiang," deals with the evolution of firearms more broadly than Fang's essay. Among Western works, see also Eloise Talcott Hibbert, *Jesuit Adventure in China: during the Reign of K'ang Hsi*, and George H. Dunne, *The Jesuits in China in the Last Days of the Ming Dynasty*, a doctoral dissertation at the University of Chicago (1944).

For sources on scientific subjects see Cyrus H. Peake, "Some Aspects of the Introduction of Modern Science into China," *Isis*, 63: 173–219 (Dec. 1934); Kenneth Ch'en, "Matteo Ricci's Contribution to and Influence on Geographical Knowledge in China," *Journal of the American Oriental Society*, 59: 325–359, 509 (1939); Henri Bernard, "Notes on the Introduction of the Natural Sciences," *Yenching Journal of Social Studies* 3: 220–241 (1941); and other references in the notes below. A special study of the Ming solicitation of military help from Japan is in Ishihara Michihiro, *Mimmatsu Shinsho Nihon kisshi no kenkyū*. The important translation by Louis J. Gallagher, S.J., *China in the Sixteenth Century: The Journals of Matthew Ricci: 1583–1610* (New York: Random House, 1953), 616 pp., was received too late for inclusion in our Bibliography.

NOTES

1. See Ssu-pu pei-yao edition, 1b–6.
2. See his "Chün-hsien lun," in *T'ing-lin wen-chi*, 1.6–11b.
3. *Jih-chih-lu chi-shih*, 29.26–28.
4. *T'ing-lin wen-chi*, 6.17ff. His *Jih-chih-lu* had the same aim as Ssu-ma Kuang's famous "mirror" for emperors, the *Tzu-chih t'ung-chien*.
5. *Jih-chih-lu chi-shih*, 10.5.
6. His comments on Ssu-ma Kuang's *Tzu-chih t'ung-chien*, entitled *Tu T'ung-chien lun*, are particularly famous.
7. *Tu T'ung-chien lun*, 2.11b; 11.28.
8. See *Huang-shu*, 1.1–4, "Yuan-chi" and the postface in the last two pages of the book.
9. *Tu T'ung-chien lun*, 7.16b–17; *Ssu-wen lu wai-pien*, the last page; and *Shih kuang-chuan*, 3.5.
10. See Liang Ch'i-ch'ao, *Chu Shun-shui hsien-sheng nien-p'u* (A chronological biography of Chu Shun-shui), *Yin-ping shih ho-chi*, special collection, ts'e 22.58.
11. For documentation and a general account, see L. Carrington Goodrich, *The*

Literary Inquisition of Ch'ien-lung, which also includes biographies of victims of the inquisition.

12. See Jung Chao-tsu, "Lü Liu-liang chi ch'i ssu-hsiang" (Lü Liu-liang and his ideas), *Fu-jen hsueh-chih*, 5.1–2: 1–85 (December 1936).

13. In Sun Yat-sen's third lecture in his *San-min chu-i*, on "Nationalism," he says that the Triad Society (Hung-men or San-ho-hui) had been organized by the old supporters of the Ming in the K'ang-hsi period. Although they saw that the situation was hopeless, their minds were full of nationalistic enthusiasm. They made plans to organize a secret society "to rebel against the Ch'ing and to restore the Ming." Their vision was farsighted, their thinking deep, their observation keen. Dr. Sun speaks of the Triad Society elsewhere and, having worked with its members, undoubtedly knew a great deal of its inner tradition. The following three works contain valuable source materials on the subject: J. S. M. Ward and W. G. Sterling, *The Hung Society or the Society of Heaven and Earth*; Hsiao I-shan, *Chin-tai mi-mi she-hui shih-liao* (Historical materials on modern secret societies); and Lo Erh-kang, *T'ien-ti-hui wen-hsien-lu* (Documents of the Heaven and Earth Society), including important supplements; see also Lo Erh-kang's article cited in the Sources above and Paul Pelliot's bibliography in *T'oung-pao*, 25: 444–448 (1926).

14. For a recent survey of this Jesuit activity and convenient references to the extensive work of Bernard, Pfister, and others, see Arnold H. Rowbotham, *Missionary and Mandarin: the Jesuits at the Court of China* (Berkeley, 1942).

15. See Ch'en Shou-yi, "Ming-mo Ch'ing-ch'u Yeh-su-hui-shih ti ju-chiao-kuan chi ch'i fan-ying," pp. 14–20.

16. The Chinese associates of the Jesuits may be divided into four groups: (1) those who believed in their religion and studied their science, such as Hsü Kuang-ch'i (Paul Hsü, 1562–1633) and Li Chih-tsao (Leo Li, d. 1630); (2) those who believed only in their religion and studied their science secondarily, or who were not by nature adapted to the study of science, such as Feng Ying-ching and Yang T'ing-yün (Michael Yang, 1557–1627); (3) those who studied only their science and did not believe in their religion, such as Fang I-chih (d. 1671?) and Chou Tzu-yü; (4) those who neither believed in their religion nor studied their science seriously, but occasionally associated with them, such as Ch'en Chi-ju (1558–1639) and Wang K'en-t'ang. All these people were reputable scholars.

17. In Hsieh Chao-chih's *Wu tsa-tsu*, see *Wu-hang pao-shu t'ang* edition 4.42b–43.

18. See *Ch'ü Chung-hsuan-kung wen-chi* (Collected Essays of Ch'ü Shih-ssu) pp. 4–6; and Fang Hao, "Ming-mo Hsi-yang huo-ch'i liu-ju wo-kuo chih shih-liao."

19. Chang Yin-lin, "Ming-Ch'ing chih-chi Hsi-hsueh shu-ju Chung-kuo k'ao-lueh," pp. 38–39, 61–69.

20. Reports of these conversions vary widely; the subject needs study.

21. For a pioneer study in this field, see Arthur F. Wright, "Fu I and the Rejection of Buddhism," in "Chinese Reactions to Imported Ideas, A Symposium," *Journal of the History of Ideas*, 12.1: 31–74 (January 1951).

22. Yang's work, entitled *Pu-te-i* (I could not keep silent) and Hsü Ch'ang-chih's *Sheng-ch'ao p'o-hsieh-chi* are two important collections of Chinese works antagonistic to Western ideas.

23. See Ch'üan Han-sheng, "Ch'ing-mo ti Hsi-hsueh yuan-ch'u Chung-kuo shuo," *Ling-nan hsueh-pao*, 4.2: 73–82 (June 1935).

24. See Juan Yuan, *Ch'ou-jen chuan* (Biographies of scientists, especially astronomers and mathematicians), 46.18–19, *Wen-hsuan lou ts'ung-shu* edition. See *T'oung Pao* (1904), pp. 561–596.

25. See Juan Yuan, *Tseng-tzu shih-p'ien chu-shih*. The last chapter deals with the formation and shape of the sky and the earth. On Juan's life and works, see W. Franke in *Monumenta Serica*.

26. See Ch'en Teng-yuan, "Hsi-hsueh lai-Hua shih kuo-jen chih wu-tuan t'ai-tu."

27. See *Ssu-k'u ch'üan-shu tsung-mu t'i-yao*, 107.4b, Tai-tung shu-chü edition, the entry under Li Yeh, "Ts'e yuan-hai ching."

28. Fang Hao, "Ch'ing-tai chin-i T'ien-chu-chiao so-shou Jih-pen chih ying-hsiang" (Japanese influence on the persecution of Catholicism during the Ch'ing Dynasty), in *Fang Hao wen-lu* (Essays of Fang Hao), pp. 47–65.

29. The development of Chinese mathematics down to the early thirteenth century may be characterized as the period of calculating rods (*ch'ou-suan*) because calculations were done by means of small rods called *ch'ou*. These rods were made of bamboo or other materials, 271 of which formed a set, about a handful. These were used to represent the numerals, and the calculation was done on a checkered board. The digits of each number were placed on one row of squares, and the unit column was marked off so that the decimals proceeded toward the right. Black rods represented positive numbers and red ones negative numbers. By manipulating these rods, calculations could be made from simple arithmetic to higher algebraic problems involving equations of four unknowns and to the thirteenth power. See Li Yen, *Chung-kuo suan-hsueh-shih*, pp. 63–95; and his *Chung-*

kuo shu-hsüeh ta-kang, pp. 36–39, 183–202; Yoshio Mikami, *Development of Mathematics in China and Japan*, pp. 27–31, 91–98; Chu Shih-chieh, *Ssu-yuan yü-chien*, 3.46–49b.

30. *Chi-ho yuan-pen*, translation of Euclid's *Elements of Geometry*. For other works by Westerners and Chinese on mathematics in the seventeenth and eighteenth centuries, see Li Yen, *Chung-suan-shih lun-ts'ung*, 1.149–193, and Li Yen, *Chung-kuo suan-hsüeh-shih*, pp. 184–257.

31. The school was known as Meng-yang-chai; Manchu and Chinese students of mathematics were assembled there early in the eighteenth century, during the last two decades of Emperor K'ang-hsi's reign. With the assistance of Westerners, they compiled a comprehensive work on the calendar, mathematics, and music under the collective title, *Lü-li yuan-yuan*. For further information, see biographies of Fang Pao, Ho Kuo-tsung, and Mei Wen-ting in Hummel.

32. The first scholar interested in the discovery and republication of ancient texts on mathematics was Tai Chen (1724–1777) in the 1770's. Later Juan Yuan (1764–1849), Lo Shih-lin (d. 1853), and other scholars were either interested in the history of mathematical studies or in annotating ancient texts. Juan's biographies of mathematicians, the *Ch'ou-jen chuan*, printed in 1799, included thirty-seven Europeans among a total of 280 persons. In this work, the facts about the lives of these foreigners may be questioned, but they were all treated with due deference. See the biographies of these men in Hummel; also Li Yen, *Chung-kuo suan-hsüeh-shih*, pp. 264–279.

33. See Li Yen, *suan-hsüeh-shih*, pp. 279–293; and biography of Li Shan-lan in Hummel.

34. In the Bibliography below see Teng Yü-han (Terrenz) and Wang Cheng, *Yuan-hsi ch'i-ch'i t'u-shuo lu-tsui* (European works on mechanical principles with illustrations); Sung Ying-hsing, *T'ien-kung k'ai-wu* (Natural resources utilized for manufacturing); Li Ch'iao-p'ing, *The Chemical Arts of Old China*; and the biography of Wang Cheng in Hummel, pp. 807–809.

35. Consult Ch'en Pang-hsien, *Chung-kuo i-hsüeh shih* (History of medicine in China), pp. 185–194; K. C. Wong and L. T. Wu, *History of Chinese Medicine*, p. 125 and *passim*; and biography of Pi Yuan, Hummel, pp. 622–625.

36. A summary of the cartographical contributions of the Catholic fathers is given in Wang Yung, *Chung-kuo ti-li-hsüeh shih* (History of Chinese geography), pp. 96–126, 218–19, and in Rowbotham, *Missionary and Mandarin*, pp. 264–269; see also Fang Hao, "K'ang-hsi wu-shih-pa-nien Ch'ing-t'ing p'ai yuan ts'e-hui Liu-ch'iu ti-t'u chih yen-chiu" (On the cartographic survey of the Liu-ch'iu Islands by command of Emperor K'ang-hsi in 1719), *Wen-shih-che hsüeh-pao*, no. 1: 159–197 (June 1950), and biographies of Hsüan-yeh, Ho Kuo-tsung, and Mei Ku-ch'eng in Hummel.

37. The passports (*p'iao*), also called letters patent, were first issued about 1711 as a means of control over foreigners by the Board of Ceremonies and also to protect the missionaries from molestation. See Latourette, *A History of Christian Missions in China*, pp. 157ff; Rowbotham, pp. 116, 163–64; *K'ang-hsi yü Lo-ma shih-chieh kuan-hsi wen-shu* (Documents relating to K'ang-hsi and the Tournon Legation from Rome), p. 2.

38. See Hummel, p. 917; Ch'en Yuan, "T'ang Jo-wang yü Mu Ch'en-wen"; Ch'en Yuan, "Yung-Ch'ien-chien feng T'ien-chu-chiao chih tsung-shih"; and Rowbotham, pp. 176–180.

39. See Hummel, p. 370, and Rowbotham, pp. 181–187.

40. See J. K. Fairbank and S. Y. Teng, "On the Ch'ing Tributary System"; and J. K. Fairbank, *Trade and Diplomacy on the China Coast*.

41. The title is "An Imperial Edict to the King of England." See *Ch'ing shih-lu*, Ch'ien-lung period, ch. 1435.11b–15, or *Tung-hua ch'üan-lu*, Ch'ien-lung, 118.4b–8b.

42. See Fairbank and Teng, "On the Ch'ing Tributary System," *passim*.

43. See *Huang-Ch'ing chih-kung t'u* (Illustrations of the regular tributaries of the imperial Ch'ing), 1.47.

44. See Earl H. Pritchard, "The Kotow in the Macartney Embassy to China of 1793."

45. See Feng Ch'eng-chün, *Hai-lu chu*, 73–4.

CHAPTER III. COMMISSIONER LIN'S PROGRAM FOR MEETING BRITISH AGGRESSION

SOURCES

There are few major sources on Lin Tse-hsü aside from his memorials in *Lin Wen-chung-kung cheng-shu* and in *I-wu shih-mo*, his chronological biography by Wei Ying-ch'i, and a few other items listed in Hummel and in our notes below. The article on Lin's works entitled "Lin Wen-chung-kung i-shu shu" by Ch'en Lu is worth consulting, and another article by the same author on the Opium War and Chinese weapons is also of interest. The various editions of the *Hai-kuo t'u-chih* deserve attention; for corrections of errors and supplementary information, see Sun Hao, *Hai-kuo t'u-chih cheng-shih*.

Wei Yuan was a great scholar and voluminous writer. For a list of his numerous works and certain Japanese studies of him, see Hummel. Attention should be called to Ch'i Ssu-ho's excellent article, "Wei Yuan yü wan-Ch'ing hsueh-feng," which gives a succinct summary of Wei's academic contributions. Ch'u-chin, *Tao-kuang hsueh-shu*, gives another good summary of academic conditions in the Tao-kuang period. For memorials, edicts, and letters concerning foreign policy from Han through Ch'ing, Chu K'o-ching, *Jou-yuan hsin-shu*, is a helpful source (chs. 3–4 on the nineteenth century include Lin, Tseng, Li, Tso, Kuo et al.). The most intimate view of the 1842 negotiations from the Chinese side is in Ssu-yü Teng, *Chang-hsi and the Treaty of Nanking*.

The literature, both scholarly and unscholarly, on the Opium War period is of course enormous and we will not try to indicate it here. Basic works of H. B. Morse and E. H. Pritchard on the East India Company trade, of D. E. Owen on the opium trade, and the like, will be found listed in the bibliography of John K. Fairbank, *Trade and Diplomacy on the China Coast: The Opening of the Treaty Ports, 1842–1854*, which also touches on many persons and incidents noted in the present volume. Attention should be called, among recent works, to Michael Greenberg, *British Trade and the Opening of China 1800–42*, which uses the important Jardine, Matheson and Co. archives; and, among Japanese works, to the articles of Ueda Toshio and Banno Masataka, which make use of the Chinese documents (*I-wu shih-mo*) as well as Western materials (see in Fairbank, *op. cit.*, vol. 2, bibliography). On the popular attitude toward the Opium War, see Ueda Toshio, "Ahen sensō to Shimmatsu kammin no shoshō." On the Cantonese anti-foreign movement of the 1840's, John J. Nolde has done a useful dissertation at Cornell, *The "Canton Question," 1842–1849: A Preliminary Investigation into Chinese Anti-foreignism and its Effect upon China's diplomatic Relations with the West* (1950). Further documents indicating the temper of the Cantonese anti-foreign movement of 1841–42 are available in Lo Hsiang-lin, "Ya-p'ien chan-cheng Yueh-tung i-min k'ang-Ying shih-liao hsü-lu."

NOTES

1. Cf. Sir George Sansom, *Japan. A Short Cultural History*; E. Herbert Norman, *Japan's Emergence as a Modern State*, pp. 29–35; and Sansom, *The Western World and Japan*, 105–110, and *passim*.

2. Chinese folklore about Europeans included the curious idea that, without rhubarb from China, Westerners would die of constipation. The history of this idea has not yet been thoroughly traced.

3. From IWSM-TK, 7.33–36b, enclosed in an edict of August 27, 1839 (not translated here). This source omits a postscript which appears in Lin's political writings (*Lin Wen-chung-kung cheng-shu*, part II, 4.16–20). CSL (324.25b–26) reproduces the covering edict of August 27, but not the communication here translated. An English translation (not followed here) is in the *Chinese Repository*, 8.10: 497–503 (Feb. 1840); a briefer popularized version in *ibid.*, 8.1: 9–12 (May 1839); and a Dutch translation in G. W. Overdijkink, *Lin Tse-hsü*, pp. 148–151.

4. The *Lin Wen-chung-kung cheng-shu* version is 20,283 chests.

5. Here the text of *Lin Wen-chung-kung cheng-shu* is followed; while the IWSM version is *ti*, meaning "ground."

6. See Wei Ying-ch'i, *Lin Wen-chung-kung nien-p'u*, p. 138.

7. That is, Wu Chia-pin (1803–1864); see CSK, 486.34, and CSLC, 67.58.

8. From "Lin Tse-hsü fu Wu Tzu-hsü pien-hsiu shu" (A Reply from Lin Tse-hsü to the Hanlin compiler Wu Tzu-hsü), in *Li-tai ming-jen shu-cha hsü-pien* (Letters of famous men of successive generations, supplement), 2 *chüan*, compiled by Wu Tseng-ch'i, 2A.18–19.

9. John Francis Davis, *China during the War and since the Peace*, I, 309–310.

10. The *Ssu-chou chih* is printed in the big collection, *Hsiao-fang-hu-chai yü-ti ts'ung-ch'ao*, *ts'e* 82.

11. The first 50-*chüan* edition of 1844 is used in this volume. There is also an 1847 edition published by the Yangchow Ku-wei-t'ang, and an 1852 edition by Ku-wei-t'ang.

12. See the recent study by A. Grosse-Aschhoff, *Negotiations between Ch'i-ying and Lagrené 1844–1846*; also Fortia d'Urban, *La Chine et l'Angleterre*, pp. 283–286; Henri Cordier, "La Mission Dubois de Jancigny dans l'Extrême-Orient," *Revue de l'histoire des colonies françaises*, 4:130–33, 146, 148; and Teng Ssu-yü, *Chang Hsi and the Treaty of Nanking, 1842*, pp. 88–89.

13. From Wei Yuan, *Hai-kuo t'u-chih*, first edition (1844), preface by Wei dated 1842, "three months after the barbarian ships left the River" at Nanking, i.e., December 1842; see ch. 1.1.

14. This title was given to I-shan, see Hummel, pp. 391–393.

15. The "three feudatories" (*san-fan*) comprised Wu San-kuei in Yunnan and Szechwan, Shang K'o-hsi in Canton, and Keng Ching-chung in Fukien; all of whom revolted against the Ch'ing government in the 1670's.

16. Lit., *Sha-chiao* and *Ta-chiao*.

5

17. On several occasions the British forces had proposed that if a certain sum of money were paid, a city would be saved from attack or destruction. Thus, near the end of July 1842, Yangchow was saved from attack by a ransom of $500,000. See Teng, *Chang Hsi*, pp. 12–13, 144–45.

18. From IWSM-TK, 31.15–20, "Ch'ih-kao Ying-i shuo-t'ieh."

CHAPTER IV. THE POLICY OF CONCILIATION

SOURCES

The main source on Ch'i-ying is not his book *Yueh-t'ai yü-sung* but his memorials collected in the *I-wu shih-mo* and *Shih-liao hsun-k'an*. In no. 35, pp. 291–93, of the latter series, an important memorial not included in the *I-wu shih-mo* boldly reports Ch'i-ying's difficulties with the corrupt domestic administration and the superior weapons and strategy of the West. Dr. T. F. Tsiang has published a translation under the title, "Difficulties of Reconstruction after the Treaty of Nanking"; otherwise, extracts would have been included in this volume. Dr. Tsiang suggests that "the document shows the personality of Kiying, his courage to tell the Emperor the bare truths and his real patriotism." On Hsü Chi-yü, see Hummel and the collection of Hsü's writings, *Sung-k'an hsien-sheng ch'üan-chi*, which indicates his family background and academic and political career.

On the whole period of the 1840's, including Lin Tse-hsü, Ch'i-ying, and others, Kuo T'ing-i's heavily documented *Chin-tai Chung-kuo shih* is a reservoir of source material and his bibliography is also useful. The most recent work on this period is Fairbank, *Trade and Diplomacy on the China Coast*. An informative analysis of the treaty revision negotiations of 1854 is in Banno Masataka, "Gaikō kōshō ni okeru Shimmatsu kanjin no kōdō yōshiki." Another useful recent study is by Chang Hsi-t'ung, "The earliest phase of the introduction of western political science into China."

NOTES

1. Cf. J. K. Fairbank, *Trade and Diplomacy*.

2. Cf. H. B. Morse, *International Relations of the Chinese Empire*, I, 519–525, which is, however, incorrect in dating the memorial as of 1850.

3. From IWSM-TK, 73.18–20b. We have reworked the translation by Thomas Wade in *Correspondence relative to the Earl of Elgin's Special Mission to China and Japan 1857–1859* (presented to the House of Lords by command, 1859), pp. 175–177.

4. *Ta-ts'an*, the great meal.

5. Wade: "on something of a footing of equality."

6. Wade: "Thus, according to the second of the Confucian books, should it be between the ruler and the nobles dependent on him."

7. From IWSM-HF, 25.4b–6; also in Chiang T'ing-fu (T. F. Tsiang), *Chin-tai Chung-kuo wai-chiao shih tzu-liao chi-yao*, 1.213–14. (Source for par. 5, p. 40.)

8. See the archives of the British Consulate at Amoy, Gribble's dispatch 17 of Feb. 12, and 19 of Feb. 14, 1844; also IWSM-TK, 71.19–22.

9. See the *Chinese Repository*, 13: 236 (1844), and 20: 184–194 (1851), on the "Universal Geography of Sü Ki-yü."

10. From *Ying-huan chih-lueh*, 7.43b–45. The translation in *Chinese Repository*, 20: 169–194 has faults and has not been followed here.

11. The annual revenue of the government at Peking in this period was close to forty million taels; for brief reference, see Hsiao I-shan, *Ch'ing-tai t'ung-shih*, 2.334–35.

12. From *Ying-huan chih-lueh*, 9.14–15.

CHAPTER V. THE THEORY OF SELF-STRENGTHENING

SOURCES

a. *Prince Kung and the Tsungli Yamen*

I-hsin's biography in Hummel is the starting point for material on the Tsungli Yamen. The two articles in Japanese by Banno Masataka, and Meng Ssu-ming, *The Organization and Functions of the Tsungli Yamen* (Harvard doctoral thesis, 1949), are very useful recent studies. Liu Hsiung-hsiang, *Ch'ing-chi ssu-shih-nien wai-chiao yü hai-fang*, also concerns the Yamen. Chang Chung-fu, "Tsung-li ko-kuo shih-wu ya-men chih yuan-ch'i," and Ch'en Wen-chin, "Ch'ing-tai chih tsung-li ya-men chi-ch'i ching-fei," are studies of the beginning, and of the financial resources of the new institution, respectively. The sections on the Tsungli Yamen in Liu Chin-tsao, *Ch'ing-ch'ao hsü-wen-hsien t'ung-k'ao*, and in Wu Ch'eng-chang, *Wai-chiao-pu yen-ko chi-lueh*, are brief but good. Wang Yen-wei and Wang Liang, *Ch'ing-chi wai-chiao shih-liao*, reproduce many original documents, while Ch'en T'i-ch'iang, *Chung-kuo wai-chiao hsing-cheng*, traces the administration of diplomatic affairs and Tung Hsun, *Huan-tu-wo-shu shih lao-jen nien-p'u*, gives some description of procedures in the Tsungli Yamen and the T'ung-wen Kuan. Yü-chüan Chang, "The Provincial Organs of Foreign Affairs in China," concerns an interesting and unique aspect of China's diplomacy.

b. *Feng Kuei-fen and his Essays*

For sources on Feng Kuei-fen, see the biographies, prefaces, and postfaces in the *Hsien-chih-t'ang kao* and the *Chiao-pin-lu k'ang-i*. The studies by Huang Ts'ui-po in the quarterly of the Sun Yat-sen Institute and by Momose Hiromu in *Tōa ronsō* are important aids (the latter also appears in a shortened Chinese translation in the *Chung-ho* monthly). There is an important brief memoir, *Feng Ch'ing-t'ing hsing-chuang*, prepared at the time of Feng's death; but in general he has not yet been adequately studied.

c. *The Taiping Rebels' Interest in Modernization*

The largest and possibly the best collection of source material on the Taiping Rebellion so far published is the *T'ai-p'ing T'ien-kuo* compiled by Hsiang Ta and more than ten others of the Chinese Historical Association and published in 1952 in eight volumes. Many books, documents, and manuscripts of the Taipings, of the imperial government, and of contemporary individual scholars are carefully reproduced in this work, which can replace many previous publications. Next to this is the *T'ai-p'ing T'ien-kuo shih-liao*, compiled by T'ien Yü-ch'ing and three others of the Research Institute of Humanities of the National Peking University and the National Library of Peking. This is also a very informative work. These two institutions have also compiled a valuable bibliography of reference works about the Taipings entitled *T'ai-p'ing T'ien-kuo ts'an-k'ao shu-mu*. The bibliographical sections in Kuo T'ing-i's *T'ai-p'ing T'ien-kuo shih-shih jih-chih* and S. Y. Teng's *New Light on the History of the Taiping Rebellion* are still useful. The latest important American publication is Professor E. P. Boardman's study (see note 10 below).

There are a number of recent articles, each of which takes up a certain aspect of the Taiping Rebellion, such as Vincent Yu-chung Shih, "Interpretations of the Taiping Tien-kuo by Noncommunist Chinese Writers," and Chester A. Bain, "Commodore Matthew Perry, Humphrey Marshall, and the Taiping Rebellion," both in *The Far Eastern Quarterly* (May 1951); James T. K. Wu, "The Impact of the Taiping Rebellion upon the Manchu Fiscal System," *Pacific Historical Review*, vol. 19 (August 1950), and John Foster, "The Christian Origins of the Taiping Rebellion," *The International Review of Missions*, 40: 156–167 (1951). Further research is of course constantly appearing in Chinese and Japanese. For Japanese articles by Ichiko Chūzō and others, see J. K. Fairbank and Masataka Banno, *Japanese Studies of Modern China* (to be published by the Harvard-Yenching Institute in 1954).

NOTES

1. From IWSM-HF, 71.18–27. We have presented only the major points of this important document; part of it is also given in Ch. VIII below.

2. Concerning Wen-hsiang, Robert Hart praised him as one of the "ablest, fairest, friendliest and most intelligent mandarins ever met by foreigners" (*These from the Land of Sinim*, p. 68). A. Michie described him as "the most conscientious as well as the most liberal-minded statesman that China has produced during the sixty years of foreign intercourse" (*The Englishman in China during the Victorian Era*, II, 374–75). W. A. P. Martin made the exaggerated statement that as long as Wen-hsiang lived, the entire initiative of the Yamen rested with him, and quoted him as saying, "We shall learn all the good we can from you people of the West" (*A Cycle of Cathay*, 362–63).

3. These essays also appear in his literary work, *Hsien-chih-t'ang kao*, chüan 10–11, published in 1877 without the title *Chiao-pin-lu k'ang-i*. The latter work was first published separately by his son in 1884 at Yü-chang, modern Nanchang. The number of essays and the wording in the *Hsien-chih-t'ang kao* are slightly different from those in the *Chiao-pin-lu k'ang-i*.

4. For the compilers and various editions of this work, see Hummel, p. 282; and Hiromu Momose's special study of it in *Tōa ronsō*, vol. 2 (January 1940), translated into Chinese in *Chung-ho yueh-k'an*, 3.3: 53–66 (March 1942).

5. From "Ts'ai Hsi-hsueh i," *Chiao-pin-lu k'ang-i*, 2.37–39.

6. From "Chih yang-ch'i i," *Chiao-pin-lu k'ang-i*, 2.40–44.

7. *Tsung-heng-chai*, an expert on theories of perpendicular and horizontal alliances, popular in the period of the Warring States.

8. Apparently Feng refers here to the Harris treaty of 1858 and to the *Kanrin Maru*, which sailed to San Francisco in 1860. See Chitoshi Yanaga, *Japan since Perry*, p. 116.

9. From "Shan yü-i i," *Chiao-pin-lu k'ang-i*, 2.45–47.

10. The Taiping influence on modern China is summed up in Lo Erh-kang's *T'ai-p'ing T'ien-kuo shih-kang*. On the subject of Western religious influence on the rebels, Professor E. P. Boardman has done a pioneer study, *Christian Influence upon the Ideology of the Taiping Rebellion*, published by the University of Wisconsin Press, 1952. We therefore omit here any materials on this very interesting topic.

11. Among the Taiping publications, the *T'ien-ch'ao t'ien-mu chih-tu* (The land system of the Heavenly Dynasty 1853), which outlines the Taiping political, economic, and social platforms, and Hung Jen-kan, *Tzu-cheng hsin-p'ien*, partly translated here, are the outstanding treatises on political ideology.

12. From *Tzu-cheng hsin-p'ien*, reproduced in *I-ching*, 17: 17–22 (Nov. 1936); 18: 7–11, and 19: 7–11. Our translation begins with *I-ching*, 18: 10; and we have supplied numbers to the author's series of items and translated extracts only. The original copy of Hung's work is in the Cambridge University Library, England, but there are now two reproductions of the *Tzu-cheng hsin-p'ien* in the *T'ai-p'ing T'ien-kuo shih-liao* (pp. 27–47) and *T'ai-p'ing T'ien-kuo* (II, 522–541), respectively. The proofreading in the latter is better than that in the former. The biography of Hung Jen-kan is available in Arthur W. Hummel, *Eminent Chinese of the Ch'ing Period* and also in Lo Erh-kang's *T'ai-p'ing T'ien-kuo shih-kao* (pp. 265–273). The latter work is beautifully written in the traditional style of Chinese dynastic histories and divides the material into four parts: 1) basic annals; 2) charts and tables of princes and Taiping officials; 3) monographs on their religion, social system, calendar, military organization, civil service, and other topics; and 4) biographies. This is another interesting and useful work by a leading expert.

13. Other reform proposals advanced by Hung Jen-kan included punishment of criminals only and not their families, prohibition of infanticide, prohibition of intoxicating drinks and opium, suppression of temples and monasteries, suppression of stage plays, and suppression of the sale of official ranks. Extracts from his work were translated in the *North China Herald*, Supplements to August 18 and 25, 1860.

CHAPTER VI. TSENG KUO-FAN'S ATTITUDE TOWARD WESTERNERS AND THEIR MACHINERY

SOURCES

On Tseng Kuo-fan, the most important sources are his complete collected works entitled *Tseng Wen-cheng-kung ch'üan-chi* and his diary, although the latter is difficult for Westerners to read. Wang Ting-an's *Ch'iu-ch'üeh-chai ti-tzu chi*, 32 *chüan*, is a detailed but ill-digested chronological biography of his teacher and superior; an abridged version of this work is called *Tseng Wen-cheng-kung shih-lueh*. Besides these, there are a *Tseng Wen-cheng-kung nien-p'u* and *Ta-shih-chi* or account of important events in Tseng's career; both are in the complete collection first noted above. These four works on Tseng Kuo-fan compiled by his subordinates do not, however, obviate the need for a good biography. Modern scholars have produced several studies such as Chiang Hsing-te, *Tseng Kuo-fan chih sheng-p'ing chi shih-yeh*; Hsiao I-shan, *Tseng Kuo-fan*; Wang Te-liang, *Tseng Kuo-fan chih min-tsu ssu-hsiang*; Chao Tseng-hui, *Tseng Kuo-fan yen-hsing chih t'i-hsi*; and Li Ting-fang, *Tseng Kuo-fan chi-ch'i mu-fu jen-wu*. All of these are sympathetic and appreciative of Tseng's merits, but none of them really grasps the spirit of his times or presents a living portrait. On the other hand, the communist scholar Fan Wen-lan has written a vitriolic critical biography of Tseng, sifting the evidence from a communist point of view. There are a number of articles on Tseng such as Shu An, "Hsiang-hsiang Tseng-shih i-wen," anecdotes of the Tseng family; Chang Yin-lin's commentary, "Po *Shui-ch'uang ch'un-i*," which also records anecdotes; and Tseng Shih-o, "Ou-yang Pai-yuan t'an Tseng Wen-cheng-kung i-shih," with further reminiscences. More serious are Ch'ü Hsuan-ying's notes on Tseng's diary. See also Ch'en Kung-lu's article on Tseng Kuo-fan and the Chinese navy. T'ang Ch'ing-tseng's essay on Tseng's economic ideas seems superficial, even though the writer is an economist.

In English, the works of William Hail and Gideon Ch'en (Ch'en Ch'i-t'ien) are well known. T. K. Ch'uan's article, "Tseng Kuo-fan," in the *T'ien-hsia Monthly*, is a simple account. E. H. Parker (tr.), "The Published Letters of the Senior Marquis Tseng," in the *China Review* and the desultory news entries about Tseng in the *North China Herald* for 1868–1871 are also useful. Professor Hellmut Wilhelm of the University of Washington, Seattle, has been making a special study of Tseng's thought; see his articles, "The Background of Tseng Kuo-fan's Ideology," and "The Problem of Within and Without, a Confucian Attempt in Syncretism." On the whole context of the 1860's, when Tseng was prominent, the most illuminating treatment is Mary C. Wright's forthcoming volume, *The T'ung-chih Restoration*.

For basic documents and information on the Shanghai Arsenal, see Gideon Ch'en's *Tseng Kuo-fan*; Wei Yün-kung, "Chiang-nan chih-tsao-chü chi"; Kan Tso-lin in *Tung-*

fang tsa-chih; and Chang Po-ch'u, "Shang-hai ping-kung-ch'ang chih shih-mo," in *Jen-wen* monthly. Ch'üan Han-sheng's article of 1951 is the most recent study, well documented and critical; see the bulletin of the Academia Sinica, Institute of History and Philology, XXIII, part 1 (1951).

NOTES

1. See *Tseng Wen-cheng-kung tsou-kao*, 2.12.
2. *Tseng Wen-cheng-kung nien-p'u*, 7.20.
3. See *Tseng Wen-cheng-kung shou-shu jih-chi*, *ts'e* 13, page unnumbered, 7th day, 5th month of the first year of T'ung-chih (June 3, 1862).
4. *Ibid.*, Tseng's diary, *ts'e* 30, 12th day, intercalary fourth month, in the seventh year of T'ung-chih (June 7, 1868).
5. *Ibid.*, the next page. Tseng Kuo-fan's letter to Kuo Sung-tao (*Shu-cha*, ch. 14, p. 22) also reports his good impression of the cordial reception extended to him by the foreign consuls at Shanghai; he predicts that there will be no trouble in treaty revision.
6. *North China Herald*, June 5, 1868.
7. Gideon Ch'en, *Tseng Kuo-fan*, pp. 53–54.
8. Tseng's diary, *ts'e* 15, 6th day, 12th month, in the first year of T'ung-chih (January 24, 1863).
9. Tseng's diary, *ts'e* 38, 19th day, 3rd month, in the tenth year of T'ung-chih (May 8, 1871).
10. *Tseng Wen-cheng-kung shu-cha*, 9.43.
11. *Ibid.*, 10.5b–6.
12. *Ibid.*, 10.18b–19.
13. *Ibid.*, 10.24b.
14. *Ibid.*, 10.30.
15. The Kiangnan Arsenal was first called *Chiang-nan chih-tsao tsung-chü* (Kiangnan central manufacturing bureau), then (1914) *Shang-hai chih-tsao chü*, and later (1917) *Shang-hai ping-kung-ch'ang* (Shanghai Arsenal). It occupied a space of 185 acres. During the Sino-Japanese conflict at Shanghai in 1932, machinery from the arsenal was moved to Hangchow and elsewhere.
16. From IWSM-TC, 61.27–30; *Tseng Wen-cheng-kung tsou-kao*, 33.5–8. Gideon Ch'en, in his *Tseng Kuo-fan* (pp. 48–49, 64, and *passim*), uses parts of this memorial, which we have therefore largely omitted.
17. On this whole subject, see Knight Biggerstaff, "The Secret Correspondence of 1867–1868: Views of Leading Chinese Statesmen regarding the Further Opening of China to Western Influence," *Journal of Modern History*, 22.2: 122–136 (June 1950).
18. IWSM-TC, 54.1b–4. The main ideas in this memorial were freely interpreted and criticized in the *North China Herald*, June 13, 1868.
19. In this period, Chinese commonly spoke of the "San-k'ou t'ung-shang ta-ch'en" or minister-superintendent of trade for the three ports in the north (i.e., Tientsin, Chefoo, and Newchwang, opened in 1858 and 1860) and the "Wu-k'ou t'ung-shang ta-ch'en" for the similar official in charge of the five ports in the south opened by the Treaty of Nanking.
20. From IWSM-TC, 80.11b.

CHAPTER VII. LI HUNG-CHANG AND WESTERN ARMS

SOURCES

Sources on Li are given under Chapter X.

Two further items of particular value for this chapter are Chang Ch'o-hsün, "Ch'i-shih-nien-lai Chung-kuo ping-ch'i chih chih-tsao," and Wang Te-chao, "T'ung-chih hsin-cheng k'ao."

NOTES

1. From IWSM-TC, 2.36.
2. CSL-TC, 44.41–43.
3. From *Li Wen-chung-kung p'eng-liao han-kao*, 2.46b–47.
4. See Tseng's *Shu-cha*, 11.6.
5. From IWSM-TC, 25.4–10.
6. *Cha-p'ao*, lit., "explosive cannon." This term is elliptical, referring to the explosive shells thrown by modern artillery.
7. On Ting Kung-ch'en, see Gideon Ch'en, *Lin Tse-hsü*.
8. In this period this quotation from the *I-ching* or "Book of Changes" was widely used; see the Appendix, 2.383, Legge's translation.
9. From IWSM-TC, 25.1–3.

CHAPTER VIII. INSTITUTIONS FOR LINGUISTIC AND
SCIENTIFIC STUDIES

Sources

The collection of Wo-jen's writings entitled *Wo Wen-tuan-kung i-shu* includes lecture notes expounding his Neo-Confucian ideas, diaries, and comments on administration; it constitutes an important source. Prince Kung's collected writings, *Lo Tao-t'ang shih-wen ch'ao*, however, do not have much historical value inasmuch as his poems and essays are mostly eulogies for birthday celebrations, funeral sacrifices, and the like. On the controversy between Wo-jen and Prince Kung over the adoption of Western science, neither of these collections is of much use, and we have to rely on the documents published in *I-wu shih-mo* and *Huang-ch'ao ching-shih wen-pien*.

On the T'ung-wen Kuan, the major sources include Meng Ssu-ming's *Organization and Functions of the Tsungli Yamen*; Wu Hsuan-i, "Ching-shih T'ung-wen kuan lueh-shih," in *Tu-shu yueh-k'an*; Knight Biggerstaff, "The T'ung Wen Kuan"; *T'ung-wen kuan t'i-ming lu*; *Papers Relating to Foreign Affairs, 1867*; and the recent important volume by Stanley F. Wright, *Hart and the Chinese Customs*, which describes Robert Hart's financial and administrative assistance to this educational venture, his difficulties with von Gumpach, and other revelations from the Customs archives. See also the Sources for Chapter V, above.

Notes

1. Hart's invaluable aid in these matters was, of course, seldom noted in Chinese official documents.
2. From IWSM-HF, 71.24b–25.
3. The ideas in this memorial are essentially the same as those in Feng Kuei-fen's essay, "Shang-hai she-li T'ung-wen Kuan i" (A proposal to establish a T'ung-wen Kuan in Shanghai); see *Hsien-chih-t'ang kao*, 10.18–20. A large part of this essay was also used by Feng in his chapter, "Ts'ai Hsi-hsueh i" (A discussion of the adoption of Western knowledge), in his *Chiao-pin-lu k'ang-i*, 2.37–39, translated in this volume as Doc. 8.
4. From *Li Wen-chung-kung tsou-kao*, 3.11–12.
5. A good translation of this memorial is to be found in *Papers Relating to Foreign Affairs, 1867* (Washington, 1868), I, 473–474.
6. A translation of this document is to be found in the same work, I, 474–476. See the original in IWSM-TC, 46.43–48b; also the translation in the *North China Herald*, February 9, 1867.
7. From IWSM-TC, 47.24–25.
8. From IWSM-TC, 48.1–4.
9. See *Ch'ien-Han shu*, 48.29b.

CHAPTER IX. TSO TSUNG-T'ANG AND THE FOOCHOW SHIPYARD

Sources

On Tso's career in general, see Hummel, pp. 762–767, and *Tso Wen-hsiang-kung ch'üan-chi*, including *Tso Wen-hsiang-kung nien-p'u*. On his activities in the Northwest, see Ch'in Han-ts'ai, *Tso Wen-hsiang-kung tsai hsi-pei*, a good piece of work; and Nishida Tamotsu, *Sa Sō-dō to Shin-kyō mondai*, a survey. The chief monographs in English are: W. L. Bales, *Tso Tsung-t'ang: Soldier and Statesman of Old China*; Gideon Ch'en, *Tso Tsung-t'ang, Pioneer Promoter of the Modern Dockyard and the Woolen Mill in China*; and Gideon Ch'en's "Tso Tsung-t'ang, the Farmer of Hsiang-shang," in *The Yenching Journal of Social Studies*. On Tso's financial and industrial activities, see the article by T'ang Hsiang-lung, cited in the notes below, and C. J. Stanley's doctoral dissertation at Harvard on *Hu Kuang-yung* (1951). Two magazine articles, Hsü I-shih, "Tso Tsung-t'ang and Liang Ch'i-ch'ao," and Lu Hsi-ta, "Tseng Tso hsiang-wu chi ch'i-t'a" (The disagreement between Tseng and Tso and other matters), are of some interest.

As for the Foochow Shipyard, the source materials include *Ch'uan-cheng tsou-i hui-pien*, which is a collection of memorials concerning China's shipping administration, and Wang Hsin-chung, "Fu-chou ch'uan-ch'ang chih yuan-ko," a special study. Prosper Giquel, *The Foochow Arsenal and Its Results, from the Commencement in 1867 to the End of the Foreign Directorate on the 16th February, 1874*, is a firsthand foreign account of the shipyard

Notes

1. See *Tso Wen-hsiang-kung shu-tu*, 24.52b–53.
2. *Tso Wen-hsiang-kung tsou-kao*, 59.51b.
3. *Tso Wen-hsiang-kung shu-tu*, 7.154–156. T'ang Hsiang-lung, "Min-kuo i-ch'ien

kuan-shui tan-pao chih wai-chai," *Chung-kuo chin-tai ching-chi-shih yen-chiu chi-k'an*, 3.1: 3–8 (1935). This subject has been carefully appraised by C. J. Stanley, *Hu Kuang-yung*.

4. See Ch'in Han-ts'ai, *Tso Wen-hsiang-kung tsai hsi-pei*, p. 142.

5. *Ibid.*, p. 116.

6. From *Tso Wen-hsiang-kung tsou-kao*, 18.1–6.

CHAPTER X. THE PROBLEM OF LEADERSHIP: PERSONALITIES AND INSTITUTIONS

SOURCES

Li Wen-chung-kung ch'üan-chi is the most important source on Li Hung-chang. The three biographies of him in *Ch'ing-shih-kao* and similar works are all about the same in quality, though different in detail. The biography in Hummel and the sources suggested there are extremely helpful. Liang Ch'i-ch'ao, *Ssu-shih-nien lai ta-shih chi*, is actually a very critical biography of Li Hung-chang written by a reformer who presumably had a firm basis for his criticism, but it should be used with caution. Wei Hsi-yü, *Li Hung-chang*, seems more balanced, while Li Shu-ch'un, "Li Wen-chung-kung nien-p'u," though it has reference value, does not seem equally good. Chang Ch'iung-chang, "Li Hung-chang i-shih i-shu," Hsi Yin, "Shu Ho-fei i-wen," and Ch'an-an, "Chang P'ei-lun yü Li Hung-chang," all present interesting anecdotes. Hsü I-shih's article on Li Ching-fang and Tseng Shih-o's account of the struggle between Weng T'ung-ho and Li Hung-chang are significant contributions.

As to Li's foreign policy, Ikeda Tōsen, "Itō kō to Ri Kō-shō," Wada Sei, "Ri Kō-shō to sono jidai," and Makino Kyōji, "Ri kō-shō no denki," all give brief treatments of the relations between Itō and Li. T. F. Tsiang, "Sino-Japanese Diplomatic Relations, 1870–1894," T. C. Lin, "Li Hung-chang, his Korea Policies 1870–1885," Shuhsi Hsü, *China and her Political Entity*, and Yuan Tao-feng, "Li Hung-chang and the Sino-Japanese War," are four studies of his policy in Korea written by Chinese specialists in diplomatic history. W. L. Langer also gives a critical account of Li in his *Diplomacy of Imperialism, 1890–1902*. Liu Hsiung-hsiang, *Ch'ing-chi ssu-shih-nien wai-chiao yü hai-fang*, deals with Chinese diplomacy and maritime defense. Hsiao I-shan, *Ch'ing-tai shih*, gives a popular account and his article, "Huai-chün yü Hsiang-chün chih pieh," though short, explains clearly the difference between the Anhwei and Hunan Armies.

On Li's diplomacy toward Japan, see also Su Ch'eng-chien, "Li Hung-chang i-kuan ti fan-Jih cheng-ts'e," and Chou Tzu-ya, "Li Hung-chang yü fan-Jih wai-chiao." Tseng Chi-tse, *Chin-yao ch'ou-pi*, and Tso Shun-sheng, "Chung-Jih wai-chiao shih-shang chih Li Hung-chang," both give a rather sympathetic review of Li's foreign policy. Chang Te-ch'ang, "Li Hung-chang chih wei-hsin yun-tung," and Wu Pao-chang, "Li Wen-chung-kung pai-shih-chou-nien chi-nien kan-yen," a commemoration of the one hundred and tenth anniversary of Li's birth, are also favorable surveys. T'ang Chi-ch'ing, "E tsu Lü-shun Ta-lien shih Li Hung-chang shou-hui chih cheng-chü," and the account in Wu Po (Fan Wen-lan), *Chung-kuo chin-tai shih*, are not favorable; like Tseng Kuo-fan, Li has become a favorite target in the retrospection of the new regime in China.

With regard to personnel, the classified diary of Wu Ju-lun entitled *T'ung-ch'eng Wu hsien-sheng jih-chi*, and the famous historical and social novel, *Nieh-hai hua* written by Tseng Po under the well-known pen name Tung-ya ping-fu, both have frequent references to Li and his contemporaries. Stanley Spector of the Far Eastern Institute, University of Washington, is writing a doctoral dissertation on Li Hung-chang, with special reference to his use of personnel.

The best Chinese source on Empress Dowager Tz'u-hsi is still Chang Ts'ai-t'ien, *Ch'ing lieh-ch'ao hou-fei chuan-kao*, in which the abundant interlineal notes are extremely valuable. Fang Keng-sheng's *errata* and supplement to Chang's work do not add much. Chang Ch'iung-chang, "Tz'u-hsi t'ai-hou i-shih," collects some anecdotes about her life history without indication of sources, and the same is true of the recent biography by Harry Hussey, *Venerable Ancestor*. J. O. P. Bland and E. Backhouse, *China under the Empress Dowager*, is also very informative, but must be used with caution. Mrs. Allen West Capiz of the University of Chicago is writing a doctoral dissertation on the Empress Dowager.

NOTES

1. See Li Hung-chang's letter to Governor Liu Chung-liang in 1875, in which he makes a very radical statement of policy toward Westernization and shows unusual impatience with Confucian ties, indicating his farsightedness compared with most of his contemporaries; *Li Wen-chung-kung p'eng-liao han-kao*, 15.3–5.

2. *Ibid.*, 19.43.

3. Detring became so entrenched at Tientsin as Li's protégé that the Inspector-general of Imperial Maritime Customs, Hart, could not transfer him elsewhere. See S. F. Wright, *Hart*, p. 534; and H. B. Morse, *International Relations*, III, 14, 407, and *passim*.

4. See Hummel, pp. 295–300. The most recent of many picturesque and personal accounts is Harry Hussey, *Venerable Ancestor*. No Western student has gone to work on the Empress Dowager's administration of affairs.

5. This marble barge, actually a stationary structure, appears to have antedated the Empress Dowager; possibly she added the paddle-box ornamentation.

6. From *Wen Wen-chung-kung shih-lueh*, ch. 1, biography, 12b–13.

CHAPTER XI. TRAINING STUDENTS ABROAD

SOURCES

a. *The Educational Mission to the United States*

Shu Hsin-ch'eng pioneered the study of the history of Chinese education and Chinese students abroad. His *Chin-tai Chung-kuo chiao-yü shih-liao* (Historical materials on modern Chinese education) and his *Chin-tai Chung-kuo liu-hsueh shih* (History of education of students abroad in modern China) are valuable compilations. A later work is Ting Chih-p'ing, *Chung-kuo chin-ch'i-shih-nien lai chiao-yü chi-shih*, which is an invaluable reference tool because the important educational events are chronologically arranged with indications of sources under each item. A good article in English by one of the 120 students sent to America is Yung Shang-him (Jung Shang-ch'ien), "The Chinese Educational Mission and Its Influence," which seems to have been usually neglected. The monographic studies by Thomas E. La Fargue are noted below.

b. *Students in Europe*

Regarding Chinese in Europe before 1871, Fang Hao gathered information on about 106 students, but published only thirteen of their names with brief biographical information; see his *Chung-wai wen-hua chiao-t'ung-shih lun-ts'ung*. Chang Hsing-lang, *Chung-Hsi chiao-t'ung shih-liao hui-pien*, and Hsiang Ta, *Chung-Hsi chiao-t'ung shih*, also provide fragmentary materials on early Chinese students abroad.

While this volume avoids the interesting problem of the "western" content of modern Japan's enormous influence upon China, brief note should be taken of the great possibilities for research in the field of Sino-Japanese cultural relations. Further study may indeed disclose that the foreign influence which reached China from Japan was in many ways greater than that which came directly from Western countries — for example, in the form of modern technical terminology, translations of Western works, and certain institutions. Three books by Sanetō Keishū, listed in the *Bibliography*, indicate some of the content of this research field with reference particularly to the Chinese students in Japan. The textbook by Kondō Haruo, *Gendai Chūgoku no sakka to sakuhin*, gives a bibliography of translations from Japanese into Chinese.

NOTES

1. This first educational mission has been described in Thomas E. La Fargue, *China's First Hundred*, and in his article, "Chinese Educational Commission to the United States: A Government Experiment in Western Education."

2. From *Li Wen-chung-kung i-shu han-kao*, 1.19b–22, dated June 26, 1871; the same document in the form of a memorial and with twelve regulations attached is in IWSM-TC, 82.46b–52, dated September 3, 1871.

3. On the Pin-ch'un mission, sent with Hart in 1866, and the mission of Chih-kang and Sun with Burlingame in 1867–1870, see Ch. XII below and the articles by Knight Biggerstaff; also S. F. Wright, *Hart and the Chinese Customs*, p. 327.

4. The IWSM version of this document has an extra passage here, not reproduced in Li's works.

5. See *Ch'ing-shih lieh-chuan*, 73.54.

6. See *Jen-ching-lu shih-ts'ao* (Poems of Huang Tsun-hsien), pp. 88–91.

7. *Li Wen-chung-kung p'eng-liao han-kao*, 18.31b–32.

8. *Ibid.*, 19.21.

9. *Li Wen-chung-kung i-shu han-kao*, 12.7–9.

10. CSL-KH, 130.6b.

11. From *Shih-k'o-chai chi-yen*, 2.1b–3.

12. Ma Chien-chung adds a note to the following effect: "The original draft of this letter has been lost. Marquis Tseng Chi-tse took great interest in this writing and he copied it in his diary during his ministership to England and France, so I have recopied it and kept it here. The author." With these views of 1877 we may compare Lo Wen-kan's survey article of 1924, "China's Introduction of Foreign Systems," in CSPSR.

SOURCES

In addition to the very useful entries in Hummel on the careers of Tseng Chi-tse and Kuo Sung-tao, note should be taken of the series of articles by Knight Biggerstaff, "The Ch'ung-hou Mission to France, 1870–1871," "The Establishment of Permanent Chinese Diplomatic Missions Abroad," "The Official Chinese Attitude toward the Burlingame Mission," and "The First Chinese Mission of Investigation Sent to Europe."

A great many late nineteenth-century Chinese impressions of the West have been preserved in diaries and travel accounts by minor officials and early students, collected mainly in the *Hsiao-fang-hu-chai yü-ti ts'ung-ch'ao*. These await special study. On Kuo Sung-tao, *Yang-chih shu-wu ch'üan-chi* and his autobiographical notes, *Yü-ch'ih lao-jen tzu-hsü*, are primary sources. Ch'u-chin's notes, on Kuo Sung-tao's letters omitted from his collected works, present some supplementary material. Yang Hung-lieh's three articles on early Chinese diplomatic missions, "Chi Kuo Sung-tao ch'u-shih Ying-Fa," "Chung-kuo chu-wai shih-kuan chih-tu ti chien-t'ao," and "Chung-kuo she-chih chu-I shih-kuan ti ching-kuo," are a useful series.

Tseng Chi-tse's complete works, entitled *Tseng Hui-min-kung i-chi*, are well worth consulting by students of modern history. His *Chin-yao ch'ou-pi* might deserve an English translation as indicating the basis of his diplomatic talent. Han Shao-su, "T'an Tseng Chi-tse," also deals with his diplomatic service. Tseng's diary recording his Western experience is in his collected writings as well as in the *Hsiao-fang-hu-chai yü-ti ts'ung-ch'ao*, *ts'e* 78, entitled *Shih-Hsi jih-chi* and covering the period from August 25, 1878, to November 14, 1886. In the same collection, *ts'e* 58, there is also a diary of Tseng Chi-tse, entitled *Ch'u-shih Ying-Fa jih-chi*, which begins September 26, 1878, and ends April 17, 1879, recording his mission to England and France. While the content of these two diaries is largely the same on the years they both cover, the *Ch'u-shih Ying-Fa jih-chi* has more entries and gives fuller information for its shorter period.

NOTES

1. See Biggerstaff, "Permanent Chinese Missions," p. 6.
2. From IWSM-TC, 27.25–26b. With Prince Kung were, of course, associated in this memorial the other members of the Yamen.
3. Translated from Wheaton's *Elements of International Law*. The published title was *Wan-kuo kung-fa* (4 *chüan*, Peking, 1864). For Martin's account, see *A Cycle of Cathay*, pp. 293–327; also S. F. Wright, *Hart and the Chinese Customs*, pp. 328–331.
4. The following passage, up to footnote 5, is translated in T. F. Tsiang's note, "Bismarck and the Introduction of International Law into China," CSPSR 15: 98–101 (1931). Our version is more literal.
5. End of passage noted in 4.
6. The following passage, to 7, is also from Tsiang's note.
7. End of passage noted in 6.
8. From *Yang-chih shu-wu wen-chi*, 11.1–11.
9. This Academy was established in 1875 in the British concession with a small museum. It was sponsored by Hsü Shou and Dr. John Fryer and financed by contributions of Western and Chinese businessmen. It was closed after 1912. See *Shang-hai-shih t'ung-chih-kuan ch'i-k'an*, 2: 513 (1933).
10. On Stephenson's plans for China, see P. H. Kent, *Railway Enterprise in China*.
11. Tseng Chi-tse's negotiations are recorded in considerable detail in his *Chin-yao ch'ou-pi*, 4 *chüan*, which gives a full account of the Sino-Russian conferences held from August 4, 1880, to February 23, 1881.
12. See Kuo Sung-tao, *Yang-chih shu-wu wen-chi*, 11.3b; Shu An, "Hsiang-hsiang Tseng-shih i-wen," *Jen-chien-shih*, 26.12; and Chin Liang, *Chin-shih jen-wu chih* (A gazetteer of modern personages), pp. 142–43.
13. From *Tseng Hui-min-kung shih-Hsi jih-chi*, 1.1–7. Tseng Chi-tse's diary was made popular by publication of a few extracts. One was by J. N. Jordan in *The China Review*, 11: 135–146 (July 1882 to June 1883), and also in the *Nineteenth Century*, 14: 989–1002; another was by the Rev. A. P. Parker in the *Chinese Recorder*, 22.7: 297–304 (July 1, 1891), and 22.8: 345–353 (August 1891). The passage translated above is also available in a French version by A. Vissière as "L'audience de congé de M. Tseng à Pekin (1878)" in *Revue d'Histoire Diplomatique*, 16: 176–186 (1902). Since this journal is not readily available, we have thought it worth while to give an English translation here.
14. Chinese used to divide a day and night into twelve periods, each of which occupied two hours. Thus, the *tzu* period is 11 P.M. to 1 A.M.; *ch'ou*, 1–3 A.M.; and *yin*, 3–5 A.M., etc.
15. The two Empress Dowagers were still acting jointly at this time, but the Tung-t'ai-hou (the Empress Dowager Tz'u-an, 1837–1881) usually kept silent.

16. Here the oral decree (*chih*) was a statement of advice or an order for Tseng Chi-tse to follow, or merely a remark, but in any case, an imperial idea, which needed no answer.

17. As noted above, Margary, an interpreter in the British service on a mission from Burma to the Yunnan frontier, was murdered on February 21, 1875. This murder provided the occasion for the Chefoo Agreement. See H. B. Morse, *International Relations*, II, 286–87.

18. That is, the "Tientsin Massacre" of 1870. The alleged kidnapping of children by the French Sisters of Charity was the cause of the attack. A Chinese mob destroyed a Roman Catholic orphanage and adjoining church and killed the French consul, two priests, ten nuns, three Russians and some thirty Chinese servants.

CHAPTER XIII. PROBLEMS OF INDUSTRIALIZATION

SOURCES

The subject of China's industrial development in the nineteenth century is fairly well documented, but little studied. Works noted in Fairbank and Liu, *Modern China*, deal principally with the twentieth century, but include recent monographs which survey the nineteenth century also.

For a bibliography of sources on Chinese railway problems, see *Chung-kuo t'ieh-tao wen-t'i ts'an-k'ao tzu-liao*, compiled by Mai Chien-tseng and Li Ying-chao. On the history of Chinese railways, there are several volumes: Tseng K'un-hua, *Chung-kuo t'ieh-lu shih*; Chang Hsin-ch'eng, *Chung-kuo hsien-tai chiao-t'ung shih*; and Chang Kia-ngau, *China's Struggle for Railroad Development*. Wang Ch'in-yü, "Pai-nien-lai Chung-kuo t'ieh-lu shih-yeh," is a useful brief account. P. H. Kent, *Railway Enterprise in China*, is still of value. Liu Ming-ch'uan's memorials, *Liu Chuang-su-kung tsou-i*, contain much valuable source material on railroad problems, as do the memorials of Sheng Hsuan-huai for a later period (see Ch. XXI).

On Chinese industrial development, several articles in the memorial volume, *Tsui-chin chih wu-shih nien*, prepared by the *Shen-pao* newspaper office, though not necessarily always of value, were nevertheless written by recognized authorities or government officials concerned with the various branches of industry. The best work on the cotton textile industry is the recent volume by Yen Chung-p'ing, *Chung-kuo mien-yeh chih fa-chan*. Kung Chün, *Chung-kuo hsin-kung-yeh fa-chan-shih ta-kang*, is a somewhat sketchy survey by periods of the general development of Chinese industry. In general, compilations of economic source material far exceed the number of critical studies yet made. Wang Kuang, *Chung-kuo hang-yeh lun*, is the best available work on Chinese shipping; Hsieh Pin, *Chung-kuo yu-tien hang-k'ung shih*, is an informative work mainly on the history of the post, telegraph, and aviation. Tezuka Masao, *Shina jūkōgyō hattatsu shi*, a history of the development of China's heavy industry, Hirase Minokichi, *Kindai Shina keizai shi*, on late Ch'ing economics, Haga Takeshi, *Shina kōgyō shi*, a history of Chinese mineral industry, and the *Shina kōsan shigen bunken mokuroku*, a bibliography of literature on Chinese natural resources compiled by the South Manchurian Railway, are a few out of the large number of Japanese works on Chinese industry and economics. Ellsworth Carlson has done a pioneer study of the K'ai-p'ing mines as a doctoral dissertation at Harvard (1952). Rhoads Murphey's volume, *Shanghai, Key to Modern China* (developed from a Harvard dissertation) is an historical-geographical study.

The "*kuan-tu shang-pan*" system has been relatively neglected.

NOTES

1. Chang Kia-ngau, *China's Struggle for Railroad Development*, p. 24.
2. *Li Wen-chung-kung tsou-kao*, 40.41.
3. From Li's memorial dated June 29, 1872, "Ch'ou-i chih-tsao lun-ch'uan wei-k'o ts'ai-ch'e che" (Planning the construction of steamships should not be given up), *Li Wen-chung-kung tsou-kao*, 19.44–50.
4. *Ibid.*, 38.16–17.
5. See Mu Hsiang-yueh, "Chung-kuo mien-yeh fa-ta shih," in *Tsui-chin chih wu-shih nien*, p. 1.
6. See Sheng Hsuan-huai's biography in *Yü-chai ts'un-kao*, 1.5–9.
7. THL-TK, 32.18.
8. See Liu Chin-tsao, *Ch'ing-ch'ao hsü wen-hsien t'ung-k'ao*, ch. 361.11,045.
9. According to the author's preface, an early version of this book had been published in Kiangsu as far back as 1862 under the title, "Important suggestions for the salvation of the time" (*Chiu-shih chieh-yao*), and later reprinted in Japan. In 1871 a second

version with a supplement, issued under the title "On change" (*I-yen*), with a preface by Wang T'ao (see Ch. XV b), was circulated in Japan and Korea. A revised edition of this book, *I-yen*, was published in 1875. The last version, *Sheng-shih wei-yen*, came out in 1893 (preface dated 1892), and was twice revised by the author and his friends *ca.* 1896 and 1899.

10. See Hsiao San, *Mao Tse-tung t'ung-chih ti ch'ing shao-nien shih-tai*, 13.

11. See ch. 2, section on women and education, especially pp. 31–33; ch. 3, on law, prison conditions, and opium smoking; and ch. 8, on agriculture, reclamation work, and poor relief.

12. From *Sheng-shih wei-yen*, 5.7b–9.

13. *Ibid.*, 1.47–48.

14. *Ibid.*, 1.52–54.

15. See Wang Ch'in-yü, "Pai-nien-lai Chung-kuo t'ieh-lu shih-yeh," *Hsueh-lin*, 2.40.

16. See *Technological Trends and National Policy, including the Social Implications of New Inventions* (Washington, D.C.: U.S. Government Printing Office, 1937), pp. 40–41.

17. Liu Ming-ch'uan's memorial and supporting statements by Li Hung-chang and Liu K'un-i would be included in this volume were they not translated in James Harrison Wilson's *China, Travels and Investigations in the "Middle Kingdom,"* pp. 126–135, 135–154, and *passim*.

18. From *Kuang-hsü cheng-yao*, 2.23. Wu Yuan-ping (Wu Ju-lun) was a co-memorialist, although for brevity only Shen Pao-chen's name is given in our title. Wu's diary (5.18) states that he drafted the memorial.

19. From *Yung-an wen-pien*, 2.9b–15.

CHAPTER XIV. THE ATTEMPT AT A POSITIVE FOREIGN POLICY

SOURCES

Documents on late Ch'ing foreign relations are listed in Fairbank and Liu, *Modern China*, section 5.1, and in Fairbank, *Ch'ing Documents*. Sources on the Chinese navy include the sections in *Huang-ch'ao cheng-tien lei-tsuan* and *Ch'ing-ch'ao hsü wen-hsien t'ung-k'ao*, and Ch'ih Chung-hu's account, "Hai-chün ta-shih chi"; see also *Ch'ing-shih kao* and the regulations of the Peiyang Navy, compiled in 1888 by the Chung-kuo tsung-li hai-chün ya-men. Although there are a few special studies of the modern Chinese army, the history of the navy seems to have been largely neglected.

The reasons for the failure at self-strengthening have been discussed by Hu Shih, Kuo Mo-jo, and many others; summary analyses are available, for example, in E. H. Norman, *Japan's Emergence as a Modern State*, and various textbooks, but no monographs have yet appeared on this subject.

On the Sino-Russian secret treaty, apart from sources mentioned above, reference may be made to Men-se t'an-hu k'o [pseudonym], *Chin-shih Chung-kuo mi-shih*, 1.224–239; Ch'en Fu-kuang, *Yu Ch'ing i-lai chih Chung-E kuan-hsi*; Liu Hsiung-hsiang, *Ch'ing-chi shih-nien chih lien-E cheng-ts'e*; Shen Chien, "Ssu-shih-yü-nien ch'ien chih lien-E wai-chiao"; and Wang Yun-sheng, "Chung-E mi-yueh pien-wei." The last article tries to prove that the Cassini Convention, another secret agreement said to have been signed in Peking on September 30, 1896, is spurious, while stating that the authenticity of the secret treaty translated in this volume is beyond doubt. The definitive work on the policies of Li Hung-chang and others in this period has been done by two leading Japanese historians, Tabohashi Kiyoshi, *Nisshin seneki gaikōshi no kenkyū*, to 1895, and Yano Jin'ichi, *Nisshin ekigo Shina gaikōshi*, on the decade following.

NOTES

1. *Li Wen-chung-kung p'eng-liao han-kao*, 12.14; see also 14.4 and *passim*.

2. *Li Wen-chung-kung tsou-kao*, 24.26.

3. Li's *P'eng-liao han-kao*, 14.29b–30.

4. Li's *I-shu han-kao*, 17.8b–9.

5. *P'eng-liao han-kao*, 19.33b–34.

6. *Ibid.*, 19.16b.

7. *Ibid.*, 19.42b–43.

8. From *Kuo Shih-lang tsou-shu*, 12.37–47.

9. See John L. Rawlinson, "The Lay-Osborn Flotilla: Its Development and Significance," *Papers on China, from the Regional Studies Seminars*, 4: 58–73 (1950).

10. For documents, see *Huang-ch'ao cheng-tien lei-tsuan*, 342.1–7.

11. See the imperial order in *Kuang-hsü cheng-yao*, 4.4, and the translation in C. B. Malone, *History of the Peking Summer Palaces*, pp. 197–98.

12. Cf. Li Chien-nung, *Chung-kuo chin-pai-nien cheng-chih shih*, 1.154–55.

13. From Chang P'ei-lun, *Chien-yü chi*, 4.2–6. The memorial was submitted on May 19, 1884.

14. From Wang Yun-sheng, *Liu-shih-nien lai Chung-kuo yü Jih-pen*, 2.261–62. Wang's source has not been located.

15. From *Ch'ing-chi wai-chiao shih-liao*, 115.20–21.

16. *Ibid.*, 116.35b–37.

17. *Ibid.*, 122.1–2b. An English translation, "from the French text of the original consulted in the Archives of the Narcomindiel (Foreign Office) at Moscow," is printed on pp. 365–366 of Victor A. Yakhontoff, *Russia and the Soviet Union in the Far East* (New York: Coward-McCann, 1931), 454 pp.

18. The Chinese word in the text here is *yueh*, "month," which is stated in the *errata* of the source to be a misprint.

CHAPTER XV. PROMOTERS OF INSTITUTIONAL CHANGE

SOURCES

On the missionary movement the standard works are those of K. S. Latourette. R. Loewenthal, *The Religious Periodical Press in China*, R. S. Britton, *The Chinese Periodical Press 1800–1912*, and Chang Hsing-lang, *Ou-hua tung-chien shih*, supply much valuable information. E. R. Hughes, *The Invasion of China by the Western World*, G. H. Danton, *The Culture Contacts of the United States and China*, J. S. Dennis, *Christian Missions and Social Progress*, and C. K. Wu, *The International Aspect of the Missionary Movement in China*, are also useful for this topic. Timothy Richard's journal, *Hsi-to*, which contains several important essays on the reform movement; Chung-ying (ed.), *Yang-wu hsin-lun* (New essays on foreign affairs), which was actually written by Richard, Allen, and others; Fu Lan-ya (John Fryer), *Tso-chih ch'u-yen* (Some advice on how to rule) —these are all selections of the writings in Chinese by influential missionaries. For a list of other missionary works and of Western books translated into Chinese in the nineteenth century, see Wylie's *Memorials of Protestant Missionaries to the Chinese*; Liang Ch'i-ch'ao, *Hsi-hsueh shu-mu piao*; and Chao Wei-hsi, *Hsi-hsueh shu-mu ta-wen*. For a bibliography of Chinese source materials on missionary problems, see Wu Sheng-te and Ch'en Tseng-hui, *Chiao-an shih-liao pien-mu*. The studies of important missionaries include W. A. Candler, *Young J. Allen*; Lee Shiu-keung, *Timothy Richard and the Reform Movement in China*; W. E. Soothill, *Timothy Richard of China*; E. W. Burt, "The Centenary of Timothy Richard," and his other article, "Timothy Richard: His Contribution to Modern China," E. W. Price Evans, *Timothy Richard*; and the recent attack from Peking by Ting Tse-liang.

Primary sources on Wang T'ao are the *T'ao-yuan wen-lu wai-pien*, *T'ao-yuan ch'ih-tu*, *Man-yu sui-lu*, *Fu-sang yu-chi*, *Hsi-hsueh chi-ts'un*, among other works written or compiled by him. Among the many studies of, or references to, Wang T'ao, the following list may be of some help: Ch'en Chen-kuo, "Ch'ang-mao chuang-yuan Wang T'ao"; Ko Kung-chen, *Chung-kuo pao-hsueh shih*; Hu Shih, *The Chinese Renaissance*; Lin Yutang, *A History of the Press and Public Opinion in China*; Chao I-ch'eng, "Wang T'ao k'ao-cheng"; Hsieh Hsing-yao, *T'ai-p'ing T'ien-kuo ts'ung-shu*; Lo Erh-kang, *T'ai-p'ing T'ien-kuo shih ts'ung-k'ao*, and *T'ai-p'ing T'ien-kuo wen-yuan*; *Wen-hsien ts'ung-pien*, no. 20; Ssu-yü Teng, *New Light on the History of the Taiping Rebellion*; Sanetō Keishū, "Wang T'ao ti tu-Jih ho Jih-pen wen-jen," translated by Chang Ming-san in *Jih-pen yen-chiu*.

Sources on Hsueh Fu-ch'eng are in *Yung-an ch'üan-chi* (Complete works of Yung-an), which includes his collected essays, *Yung-an wen-pien*, and two supplements, *Yung-an wen hsü-pien* and *Yung-an wen wai-pien*; as well as *Hai-wai wen-pien*, *Ch'u-shih tsou-su*, *Ch'u-shih kung-tu*, *Ch'ou-yang ch'u-i*, and *Ch'u-shih Ying-Fa-I-Pi ssu-kuo jih-chi*. These works as put together in the *Yung-an ch'üan-chi* are convenient to use, but there are some typographical errors and the text is not as legible as in punctuated block-print editions of the above works (the diary, the official dispatches, and the two supplements to his essays), all of which were separately published by Ch'uan-ching-lou. In addition, the *Yung-an pi-chi* (Desultory notes of Yung-an), jotted down during the years 1865–1891 and printed in 1895 in several editions, is a work of historical and scholarly value. See also *Ch'ing-shih kao*, ch. 452; *Pei-chuan-chi pu*, ch. 13; *Ch'ing-shih lieh-chuan*, ch. 58; Hummel, *Eminent Chinese*, pp. 331–32; Huang Yen-yü, "Viceroy Yeh Ming-ch'en and the Canton Episode (1850–1861)", *Harvard Journal of Asiatic Studies* 6.1. We are of course much indebted to the account by Tu Lien-che in Hummel, cited above.

It is obvious that the above materials, as well as the extensive writings of missionaries in Chinese, have hardly been studied in the West.

1. R. S. Britton, *The Chinese Periodical Press*, p. 53.
2. This introductory note is supplementary to the biography by Roswell S. Britton in Hummel, *Eminent Chinese*. Wang T'ao had several names: Wang Li-pin, Huang T'ao, Huang Wan, Chung-t'ao, T'ien-nan tun-sou, etc.
3. Under the title, *T'ao-yuan wen-lu wai-pien*.
4. *Ibid.*, 2.5–7.
5. *Ibid.*, 2.11b–14.
6. *Ibid.*, 3.12–14.
7. *Ibid.*, 3.12–17; 25b–27b.
8. *Ch'u e-wai ch'üan-li*, 3.27b–29.
9. *T'ao-yuan wen-lu wai-pien*, 4.22.
10. *Ibid.*, 1.1. This idea was used most effectively by K'ang Yu-wei; see Chapter XVI.
11. *Ibid.*, 1.2.
12. *Ibid.*, 1.21b–23.
13. "Shang tang-lu lun shih-wu shu," a letter submitted to the authorities discussing current affairs, *ibid.*, 10.20b–22.
14. "Yuan-hsueh," *ibid.*, 1.2b–3b.
15. A letter to Hsü Chün-ch'ing (Hsü Yu-jen) in *T'ao-yuan ch'ih-tu*, 4.21b–22.
16. "Pien-fa," parts B and C, *T'ao-yuan wen-lu wai-pien*, 1.13–17.
17. "Chih-chung," *ibid.*, 1.25–26.
18. "Chi Ying-kuo cheng-chih," *ibid.*, 4.17.
19. See *Ch'u-shih . . . jih-chi*, 4.12b.
20. *Ibid.*, 3.25b–26b.
21. *Ibid.*, 2.6; 3.34–35; 6.15b–16b.
22. *Ibid.*, 5.16.
23. See *Ch'u-shih kung-tu*, preface, p. 2.
24. From *Ch'ou-yang ch'u-i*, 1.29b–32.
25. From *Ch'u-shih Ying-Fa-I-Pi ssu-kuo jih-chi*, 2.5b–6.
26. Hsueh also refers here to I I or Hou I, a famous archer who attempted to attack Hsia, but was killed by Han-cho. See Ssu-ma Ch'ien, *Shih-chi*, 2.23b n; and 67.15b.
27. Kings Chieh of Hsia, Chou of Shang, and Yu and Li of Chou were all notorious tyrants.
28. From *Ch'u-shih . . . jih-chi*, 2.11b–12.
29. Wu Ch'en, a native of Ch'u, once tried to stop the struggle between Prince Ch'u-hsiang and another person for a beautiful woman. Later on, Wu Ch'en got the woman for himself and fled with her to the state of Wu. For this, all the members of his family in Ch'u were killed. Wu Ch'en taught the Wu state to fight against Ch'u and caused the latter much trouble. See Ssu-ma Ch'ien, *Shih-chi*, 39.31.
30. From *Ch'u-shih . . . jih-chi*, 6.2.
31. From *Hai-wai wen-pien*, 3.8b–9.

CHAPTER XVI. K'ANG YU-WEI AND HIS ASSOCIATES

SOURCES

General accounts of the Reform Movement of 1898 include Meribeth E. Cameron, *The Reform Movement in China*, a pioneer survey which uses rather few Chinese sources; a scholarly article by Ho Ping-ti, "Weng T'ung-ho and the 'One Hundred Days of Reform,'" which clarifies Weng's role in the movement; Albert Maybon, *La Politique Chinoise, 1898–1908*, which is probably the best French work on the period; Alfred Forke, *Geschichte der neueren chinesischen Philosophie*, which considers K'ang, Liang and others; Wolfgang Franke, "Die Staatspolitischen Reformversuche K'ang Yu-weis und seiner Schule. Ein Beitrag zur geistigen Auseinandersetzung Chinas mit dem Abendlande," a dissertation with ample documentation; Hsiao Kung-ch'üan, *Chung-kuo cheng-chih ssu-hsiang shih*, which is probably the best treatment in Chinese of the political thought of K'ang and his associates. Joseph R. Levenson, *Liang Ch'i-ch'ao and the Mind of Modern China* (Harvard University Press, 1953), and his article, "The Breakdown of Confucianism: Liang Ch'i-ch'ao before Exile — 1873–1898," in the *Journal of the History of Ideas* (October 1950) are recent analytic studies of Liang and his ideas. So Kwan-wai, *Western Influence and the Chinese Reform Movement of 1898*, a doctoral dissertation at the University of Wisconsin (1950), is a workmanlike study.

A considerable amount of research on the Reform Movement has been done in Japan by a number of competent scholars: Murakami Tomoyuki, *Bojutsu seihen shiwa*, is a comprehensive study of the movement. It is also dealt with in the article by Sanetō Keishū, "Kindai Shina to gairai shisō" (in *Kindai Shina shisō*); in Fujiwara Sadamu,

Kindai Chūgoku shisō; and Ojima Sukema, *Chūgoku no kakumei shisō*, although all of these cover a broader scope. The first chapter of Yano Jin'ichi, *Shinchō matsu-shi kenkyū*, is a careful research into many aspects of the events of 1898, and another critical appraisal is Inada Masatsugu's article, "Bojutsu seihen ni tsuite" (in *Kindai Chūgoku kenkyū*). In the same volume is a detailed and critical analysis of the origin, nature, and influence of K'ang Yu-wei's conception of the "Great Harmony" (*Ta-t'ung ssu-hsiang*) by Itano Chōhachi, who has also written an appraisal of Liang Ch'i-ch'ao's idea of it, along the same lines, in the *Festschrift* for Dr. Wada Sei. A careful and independent analysis of the whole current of reform and intellectual change is provided in three articles by Onogawa Hidemi, "Shimmatsu yōmuha no undō"; "Shimmatsu no shisō to shinkaron"; and "Shimmatsu hempōron no seiritsu." The second describes the influence of Yen Fu's translation of Huxley's *Evolution and Ethics* on the reformers of the period. K'ang and the failure of 1898 are also dealt with in two chapters of Izushi Yoshihiko, *Tōyō kinseishi kenkyū*.

The philosophy of K'ang, T'an, and their group is briefly treated in many surveys in English, such as Lin Mou-sheng, *Men and Ideas*, Feng Yu-lan, *A Short History of Chinese Philosophy*, and Tseng Yu-hao, *Modern Chinese Legal and Political Philosophy*. The extensive Chinese periodical literature includes the following articles: Ch'en Kung-lu, "Chia-wu-luan hou keng-tzu-luan ch'ien Chung-kuo pien-fa yun-tung chih yen-chiu"; Chih Kuei, "Ch'ing-tai K'ang-Liang wei-hsin yun-tung yü ko-ming-tang chih kuan-hsi chi ying-hsiang"; I-shih, "Jung-lu yü Yuan Shih-k'ai"; Mei Ying, "Wu-hsü cheng-pien chen-wen"; the *Ta-kung-pao* article, "Kuan-yü wu-hsü cheng-pien hsin shih-liao"; Wu Tse, "Wu-hsü cheng-pien yü hsin-chiu tang-cheng" and "Pao-huang-tang yü K'ang-Liang lu-hsien"; and "Lun pien-fa chih ching-shen," an editorial in *Tung-fang tsa-chih*, no. 7 (1904).

On K'ang Yu-wei, apart from his own writings, there are several biographies: Liang Ch'i-ch'ao, *K'ang Nan-hai chuan*; Chang Po-chen, *Nan-hai K'ang hsien-sheng chuan*; and Chao Feng-t'ien, "K'ang Ch'ang-su hsien-sheng nien-p'u kao." Mr. Chao has specialized on K'ang and Liang; much of his material is still in manuscript. See also Wu Tse, *K'ang Yu-wei yü Liang Ch'i-ch'ao*. For a good edition of K'ang's *Ta-t'ung shu*, see the one compiled by Ch'ien Ting-an and published by the Chung-hua Book Co. in 1932. The commonly available edition, in *Wan-mu ts'ao-t'ang ts'ung-k'an* and in *K'ang Nan-hai wen-ch'ao*, is incomplete.

On Liang Ch'i-ch'ao, apart from his own voluminous writings (see Bibliography) and the studies of him mentioned above, there are several biographical sketches or brief studies in Chinese of his ideas and influence: Liu P'an-sui, "Liang Jen-kung hsien-sheng chuan," Chang Ch'i-yun, "Liang Jen-kung ssu-hsiang pieh-lu," and Su Ch'ih (Chang Yin-lin), "Chin-tai Chung-kuo hsueh-shu-shih shang chih Liang Jen-kung." Wu Ch'i-ch'ang's *Liang Ch'i-ch'ao* seems to be an unfinished job published posthumously, but it presents a framework for Liang's biography. Wu was one of Liang's best students.

On T'an Ssu-t'ung, *T'an Liu-yang ch'üan-chi*, *Jen-hsueh*, published in *Ch'ing-i-pao*, and *T'an Ssu-t'ung shu-chien*, compiled by Ou-yang Yü-ch'ien, are primary sources. Ts'ai Shang-ssu, "T'an Ssu-t'ung hsueh-shu ssu-hsiang t'i-yao," and Hu Yuan-chün, "T'an Ssu-t'ung *Jen-hsueh* chih p'i-p'ing," are special studies of considerable value.

On Yen Fu, there are the following books and articles in Chinese: a biography by Wang Shen-jan, in his *Chin-tai erh-shih-chia p'ing-chuan*; Lin Yao-hua, "Yen Fu she-hui ssu-hsiang," in *She-hui hsueh-chieh*; Wang Chü-ch'ang, *Yen Chi-tao nien-p'u*; Kuo Pin-ho, "Yen Chi-tao"; and two articles by Chou Chen-fu, "Yen Fu ssu-hsiang chuan-pien chih p'ou-hsi" and "Yen Fu ti Chung-Hsi wen-hua kuan."

NOTES

1. Such as T'ang Chen, *Wei-yen*, published in 1890, and Cheng Kuan-ying, *Sheng-shih wei-yen* (see Chapter XIII a). Two other works of the same nature were *Hsin-cheng chen-ch'üan* (The true meaning of new government), written by Hu Li-yuan, who was trained in England, and Ho Ch'i, who graduated *cum laude* from the British college in Hongkong; and Ch'en Chih, *Yung-shu*. Ch'en was influenced by his frequent visits to Hongkong and Macao, and advocated a higher social position for the merchant class and thorough reform along the lines of Western government. He also warned against the ambitions of Russia in China.

2. *Kung-ch'e shang-shu chi*; see the lithographic edition, published in Shanghai, 1895. (Correction: On p. 148, *for* see Ch. xvi *read* see Ch. xviii.)

3. See Liang Ch'i-ch'ao, *Ch'ing-tai hsueh-shu kai-lun*, pp. 56–57.

4. See *Jen-ching-lu shih-ch'ao*, Peiping, 1930.

5. See Wen T'ing-ching, "Huang Tsun-hsien chuan"; also Ko Hsien-ning, "Chin-tai Chung-kuo min-tsu shih-jen Huang Kung-tu."

6. Ko Hsien-ning, *ibid.*, p. 101.

7. Such as *Papers from a Viceroy's Yamen* (1901) and *The Story of a Chinese Oxford Movement* (1910). He also wrote in German.

18

8. See Wen Yuan-ning, "Ku Hung-ming," in *T'ien-hsia Monthly*. There are also many anecdotes and biographies of Ku in Chinese as well as a collection of his essays entitled *Tu I ts'ao-t'ang wen-chi*.

9. See R. S. Britton, *The Chinese Periodical Press 1800–1912*, p. 97.

10. *Yen Chi-tao wen-ch'ao*, 2.19.

11. *Ibid.*, 1.1b.

12. *Ibid.*, 4.19b.

13. Letters 58–59, from Yen Fu's correspondence in *Hsueh-heng*, no. 18: 6–7 (1923).

14. From *K'ang Nan-hai wen-chi hui-pien*, 8.20.

15. From *Yin-ping-shih ho-chi*, 1.1–8.

16. See Lin's biography in *Kuo-ch'ao hsien-cheng shih-lueh*, 25.6.

17. Mai Chung-hua (comp.), *Huang-ch'ao ching-shih wen hsin-pien*, 2.19b–32.

18. From *Huang-ch'ao ching-shih wen hsin-pien*, 27.8–9. (Source for Doc. 44.)

19. See *Huang-ch'ao ching-shih wen san-pien*, 15.6–8.

CHAPTER XVII. THE REFORM PROGRAM OF CHANG CHIH-TUNG

SOURCES

Materials on Chang are indicated in Hummel, pp. 27–32. One edition of *Chang Wen-hsiang-kung nien-p'u* was compiled by Hsü T'ung-hsin, and is more informative but poorly arranged; the other, by Hu Chün, is based mainly on Hsü's work and is less informative but easier to use. See also Hsiao Kung-ch'üan, *Chung-kuo cheng-chih ssu-hsiang shih*, pp. 407–415; and the following articles: Hsieh En-hui, "Chang Hsiang-t'ao chih ching-chi chien-she,"; "Chang Wen hsiang-kung yü chiao-yü chih kuan-hsi," in *Chiao-yü tsa-chih*; L. Odontines, "Chang Chih-tung and the Reform Movement in China"; Meribeth E. Cameron, "The Public Career of Chang Chih-tung 1837–1909"; Ch'üan Han-sheng, "Ch'ing-mo Han-yang t'ieh-ch'ang" (The Han-yang iron and steel works, 1890–1908); and Wang Shou-ch'ien, "Chung-kuo chi-ch'i pan chu-tsao chih-ch'ien yü yin-yuan chih ch'i-yuan" (The beginning of machine minting of coins and silver dollars in China).

NOTES

1. *Ch'üan-hsueh-p'ien*, two *chüan*. The first, part A, is called *nei-p'ien*, and the second, part B, *wai-p'ien*. There is a rough condensed translation by Samuel I. Woodbridge (New York, 1900) entitled *China's Only Hope, An Appeal by Her Greatest Viceroy, Chang Chih-tung*, and a better French translation by Jerome Tobar (Chang-hai, 1909). There are three Chinese editions in circulation. One is in *Chang Wen-hsiang-kung ch'üan-chi*, ch. 202–203, used as the basis of the present translation. Another is in the Chien-hsi-she ts'ung-k'o punctuated edition. The third is a separate edition republished in Chekiang in 1898.

2. See pt. A, ch. 4, in *Chang Wen-hsiang-kung ch'üan-chi*, 202.16–18.

3. Pt. A, ch. 3, in the same work, 202.13–15.

4. See CSL, Te-tsung, 484.10b–11.

5. Pt. B, ch. 13, in *Chang Wen-hsiang-kung ch'üan-chi*, 203.48.

6. Preface to *Ch'üan-hsueh-p'ien*, 1b.

7. *Ibid.*, 2b.

8. Chang, *ch'üan-chi*, 202.2b–3.

9. *Ibid.*, 203.24.

10. See Chang's *nien-p'u*, compiled by Hu Chün, 3.16b.

11. See Chang's memorial in *ch'üan-chi*, 40.1–5.

12. *Ibid.*, 203.30–34.

13. From pt. A, ch. 6, "cheng-ch'üan," in Chang's *ch'üan-chi*, 202.23–26.

14. *Chiu-chou*, i.e., the political divisions cited in the chapter "Yü-kung" of the *Book of History*.

15. From pt. A, ch. 7, "Hsün-hsü," in *ch'üan-chi*, 202.27–28.

16. From pt. A, ch. 9, "Ch'ü-tu," in the same work, 202.38–40.

17. See *The Analects of Confucius*, bk. 2, ch. 3, Legge's translation.

18. Cf. F. Max Müller's translation, *The Book of Rites*, Oxford, 1885, p. 82.

19. From ch. 7, "Pien-fa," in *ch'üan-chi*, 203.19–22.

20. These words are quoted from chapters 41, "Sun," 42, "I," and the appendix, respectively, of the *Book of Changes* in order to convince scholars that there is a basis for reform in the classics.

21. See the *Book of History*, "Pan-keng," A, sec. 13.

22. See *Tso-chuan*, bk. 10, the 17th year of Duke Chao.

23. See *Analects*, bk. 2, 11.

24. *Ibid.*, bk. 6, 21.

25. See *Chung-yung*, ch. 25

26. See *Mencius*, bk. 7, pt. 1, ch. 7. Note: we have consulted and modified Legge's translation of the preceding references.

27. Quoted from *Chuang Tzu*, ch. 2, "Equality of Things and Opinions." Cf. Feng Yu-lan's translation, p. 61; i.e., they are too hasty in forming their opinions.

28. From ch. 15, "Fei kung-chiao," in *ch'üan-chi*, 203.51–53.

CHAPTER XVIII. THE FAILURE OF 1898

SOURCES

Sources for this chapter are mentioned in the notes, and under Chapter XVI. We have not seen a new compilation entitled *Wu-hsü pien-fa*, published in Peking in late 1953.

NOTES

1. On this general subject, see Ch'en Ch'iu, "Wu-hsü cheng-pien-shih fan pien-fa jen-wu chih cheng-chih ssu-hsiang," in *Yen-ching hsueh-pao*.

2. From *Nan-hai K'ang hsien-sheng chuan*, 26b–28.

3. *Tsou*, usually translated "memorialize," but meaning to present one's views to the emperor.

4. From Wang Yun-sheng, *Liu-shih-nien lai Chung-kuo yü Jih-pen*, 3.272–275. The original text is in *Zoku Itō Hirobumi hiroku* (Supplement to the collection of Itō's private documents), compiled by Hiratsuka Atsushi, pp. 126–129.

5. After this answer, the emperor asked when Itō had started his trip from Japan. Itō answered that he had started the trip from his country about a month before and had stayed more than ten days in Korea before coming to China. These lines were omitted by Wang Yun-sheng.

6. In this section, in addition to selecting a number of passages not hitherto noted, we have relied heavily on the following two articles by Ch'üan Han-sheng: "Ch'ing-mo ti Hsi-hsueh yuan-ch'u Chung-kuo shuo" and "Ch'ing-mo fan-tui Hsi-hua ti yen-lun." See also the article by Ch'en Ch'iu cited in note 1 above.

7. See Ch'en Ch'iu, pp. 82–83.

8. From Wang Hsien-ch'ien, *Hsü-shou-t'ang shu-cha*, 2.75–76, 1907 edition. (Ch'en Ch'iu, p. 98, mistakes the *shu-cha* for *wen-chi*.)

9. Ch'u Ch'eng-po was less an opponent of reform than a critic of the reformers and their methods. His memorial is in *Chien-cheng-t'ang che-kao*, 2.18–20, quoted by Ch'en Ch'iu, pp. 84–85.

10. From *Huang-shih li-shih chi*, 41.43. Cf. Ch'en Ch'iu, pp. 90–91.

11. Yeh Te-hui was another scholar who said that it was not worth while to imitate Western methods of agriculture, industry or military training. Agriculture, for example, depended upon the proper rain and sunshine, but Westerners had no way to control them. The military systems of England and Germany were good only for fighting on the sea or along the coast. See Su Yü, *I-chiao ts'ung-pien*, 4.10 and 5.28, preface dated 1898; this work is a collection of memorials and letters of conservatives attacking the reformers.

12. See Hellmut Wilhelm, "The Problem of Within and Without, a Confucian Attempt in Syncretism," *Journal of the History of Ideas*.

13. Su Yü, 2.8b, Wen-ti's impeachment of K'ang Yu-wei.

14. From *Hsiao-fang-hu-chai . . .*, *ts'e* 60.470–478.

15. *Ibid.*, *ts'e* 56.184. The diary was written in 1876–77. The *Ying-yao jih-chi* by the same author in the *Ling chien-ko ts'ung-shu* is a much abbreviated version; it was published by Chiang Piao to promote reform, so that many conservative opinions were omitted.

16. See *Shih-chiu-te-chai tsa-chu* (Miscellaneous writings of Liu Yueh-yun), *ts'e* 1, preface to "Ko-wu chung-fa," first page.

17. See *Pin-meng chi* (preface dated 1870), 2.6, in *Ch'un-tsai-t'ang ch'üan-shu*, *ts'e* 61.

18. See *Hsi-shih li-ts'e* (A glimpse into Western affairs), written *ca.* 1883, in *Hsiao-fang-hu-chai . . .*, *ts'e* 62, p. 530.

19. In Chu's *Wu-hsieh-t'ang ta-wen* (Answers to questions in the orthodox studio), 4.50, author's preface dated 1892, Cho-an ts'ung-kao edition.

20. See his *Ying-hai-lun* (A discussion of the circuit of the seas), 489b, in *Hsiao-fang-hu-chai . . .*, *ts'e* 60.

21. See his "San ta-yu lun" (On three great anxieties), *Pin-meng-chi*, 6.7b–10.

CHAPTER XIX. THE BOXER UPRISING

Sources

A very useful collection of materials on the Boxer Uprising is the four-volume work entitled *I-ho-t'uan*, compiled by Chien Po-tsan and others and published in 1951. Its annotated bibliography of 278 Chinese and Western sources dealing with the uprising, in vol. 4, pp. 529–604, supersedes others previously compiled by Ch'ü Tui-chih and Chao Hsing-kuo. Nevertheless the bibliography of Chinese materials dealing with cases involving Christian missions, compiled by Wu Sheng-te and Ch'en Tseng-hui, is still useful. Lao Nai-hsuan's three works on the Boxers, *Ch'üan-an san-chung*, are essential. Kuo Pin-chia's "Keng-tzu ch'üan-luan" is a good short account of the Boxer rebellion and its diplomatic aftermath. For an analysis of this movement by a Communist scholar, Fan Wen-lan's *Chung-kuo chin-tai shih* (pp. 403–508) may be consulted. For a recent study of the evidence, see Robert Sheeks, "A Re-examination of the I-ho Ch'üan and its Role in the Boxer Movement," *Papers on China*, 1: 74–135 (1947), and Paul A. Varg, "William W. Rockhill's Influence on the Boxer Negotiations," *Pacific Historical Review*, vol. XVIII, no. 3 (August 1949). Yano Jin'ichi's chapters on the history and nature of the Boxer Uprising in his *Shinchō matsu-shi kenkyū* (chs. 3–4, pp. 61–168) and Ichiko Chūzō's article on the nature of the Boxer movement, in *Kindai Chūgoku kenkyū* are important studies, and note should also be taken of the two articles by Yamamoto Sumiko and by Tabohashi Kiyoshi. The latter touches the question of foreign provocation.

Notes

1. These three short documents are translated from Chien Po-tsan (comp.), *I-ho-t'uan*, 4.148–49.
2. See the biographies of Hsü and Yuan in Hummel, pp. 312–13 and 945–948.
3. From *Kuang-hsü hui-yao*, 26.8b–10. These three documents are also published in *I-ho-t'uan*, 4.159–168, based on Yuan's first autographic manuscript, which is more detailed than the *Kuang-hsü hui-yao* edition. Not all scholars are convinced of their exact authenticity as reproduced in various collections, or whether they were actually presented to the throne, but there is no doubt that the general view which they put forward represents accurately what these martyred officials stood for at the time.
4. See his study of the origin of the I-ho-ch'üan, *I-ho-ch'üan chiao-men yuan-liu k'ao*, reprinted in Tso Shun-sheng, *Chung-kuo chin-pai-nien shih tzu-liao hsü-pien*, vol. A, and other collections.
5. From *Kuang-hsü cheng-yao*, 26.12b–13b.
6. *Ibid.*, 26.18b–20b.

CHAPTER XX. THE CONSERVATIVE REFORM MOVEMENT

Sources

a. *The Post-Boxer Program*

This topic has been little studied, and the material is meager and scattered. For general information, see textbooks like those of Ch'en Kung-lu, *Chung-kuo chin-tai shih*, or Li Chien-nung, *Chung-kuo chin-pai-nien cheng-chih shih*. For bibliography, see Ma Feng-chen, *Ch'ing-tai hsing-cheng chih-tu yen-chiu ts'an-k'ao shu-mu*, and *Modern China* by Fairbank and Liu. For primary materials, see such compilations as *Kuang-hsü cheng-yao*, *Hsuan-t'ung cheng-chi*, *Tung-hua-lu*, CSL and CSK; also *Tung-fang tsa-chih*, published Shanghai from 1904. The first issues of yearbooks, such as *Chung-kuo nien-chien*, or *Shen-pao nien-chien*, usually give a summary of earlier events; see S. Y. Teng and Knight Biggerstaff, *An Annotated Bibliography of Chinese Reference Works*, ch. 7, on yearbooks. Note also the writings of prominent individuals like Chang Chih-tung, Yuan Shih-k'ai, Chang Chien, and Sheng Hsuan-huai. The biography of Liang Shih-i, *San-shui Liang Yen-sun hsien-sheng nien-p'u*, is important and informative. In connection with these works, *Min-kuo t'u-chih ch'u-i* (1915) by Wu T'ing-fang (1842–1922), a diplomat and western-trained official prominent in the 1900's, may also be suggested. For the reform of China's legal codes, Dr. M. J. Meijer's monograph on the introduction of modern criminal law, which surveys the work of Shen Chia-pen and others in the decade 1901–1911 with translations of eleven key documents, is indispensable. A remarkably penetrating picture of the imperial administration of China in its last years is given in the two-volume handbook by Hattori Unokichi, *Shinkoku tsūkō*, published in 1905. The movement for a national assembly is dealt with in Onogawa Hidemi, "Shimmatsu hempōron no seiritsu."

b. *Educational Reform*

In addition to items mentioned under Chapter XI, note Chiang Shu-ko, *Chung-kuo chin-tai chiao-yü chih-tu*; Chuang Yü and Ho Sheng-nai, *Tsui-chin san-shih-wu-nien chih Chung-kuo chiao-yü*; Ch'en I-lin, *Tsui-chin san-shih-nien Chung-kuo chiao-yü shih*; and Chiang Monlin, *Tides from the West*.

c. *Constitutionalism*

The diaries of Tai Hung-tz'u, *Ch'u-shih chiu-kuo jih-chi*, and Tsai-tse, *K'ao-ch'a cheng-chih jih-chi*, are as important as the *Ou-Mei cheng-chih yao-i* from which Doc. 52 is translated. Li Chien-nung, *Chung-kuo chin-pai-nien cheng-chih shih*, has a good general discussion of this topic. Articles in *Hsien-cheng tsa-shih* (Constitutional government miscellany), 1.1, and in *Tung-fang tsa-chih*, which has a special issue on constitutional government, January–February 1907, are invaluable contemporary sources. See also P'an Wei-tung, *The Chinese Constitution: A Study of Forty Years of Constitution-making in China*, Tsao Wen-yen, *The Constitutional Structure of Modern China*, and the article by E-tu Zen Sun, "The Chinese Constitutional Missions of 1905–1906." Since there are a few English works summarizing this early constitutional history, no attempt is made in the text to sketch it in.

d. *Yuan Shih-k'ai and the Modern Army*

Shen Tsu-hsien and Wu K'ai-sheng, *Jung-an ti-tzu chi* (An account of Jung-an [Yuan Shih-k'ai] by his disciples), is actually the official biography of Yuan Shih-k'ai. Shen Tsu-hsien was also the compiler of *Yang-shou-yuan tsou-i chi-yao*, a collection of important memorials of Yuan Shih-k'ai. "Yuan ta-tsung-t'ung lueh-shih" in Shang Ping-ho, *Hsin-jen ch'un-ch'iu* (A chronicle of 1911–1912), ch. 4, contains a biographical sketch. Chu Wu, "Wo-kuo chih lu-chün," in *Kuo-feng pao*, Chiang Fang-chen, "Chung-kuo wu-shih-nien lai chün-shih pien-ch'ien shih," and Wen Kung-chih, *Tsui-chin san-shih-nien Chung-kuo chün-shih shih*, deal with military history. See also Georg Wegneuer, "Der Gouverneur von Shantung," *Deutsche Kolonialzeitung*, 27 (June 1901); and Ralph L. Powell, "The Rise of Yuan Shih-k'ai and the Pei-yang Army," *Papers on China*, 3: 225–256 (1949), which has been developed in a doctoral dissertation at Harvard. Arthur W. Hummel, Jr., *Yuan Shih-k'ai as an Official under the Manchus*, is a master of art's thesis at the University of Chicago (1949).

NOTES

1. The extensive bibliography awaiting study in this field is indicated in Fairbank and Liu, *Modern China*. See also *Bibliography of Modern Chinese Law in the Library of Congress*, compiled in 1944, which includes 501 items in Chinese and Western languages.

2. See CSL, Te-tsung, 476.8–10b.

3. *Ibid.*, 481.4b.

4. These joint products were written as follows: Liu K'un-i asked Chang Chih-tung to be the chief writer; Liu and his subordinates, Chang Chien, Shen Tseng-chih, and others, each wrote suggestions and sent them to Chang. Chang also ordered his own subordinates to offer opinions. He then put all these ideas together and edited them. Writing one or two items each day, it took him more than a month to finish the composition (see Hu Chün, *Chang Wen-hsiang-kung nien-p'u*, 4.13).

5. See CSL, Te-tsung, 486.15b.

6. *Ibid.*, 485.14, 19; and 486.6.

7. From *Tsou-i* in *Chang Wen-hsiang-kung ch'üan-chi*, 52.9b–29.

8. Cf. Legge, *The Works of Mencius*, bk. VI, pt. II, ch. 15.

9. From *Chang Wen-hsiang-kung ch'üan-chi*, 53.1–33.

10. *Ibid.*, 54.1–36.

11. See Teng Ssu-yü, *Chung-kuo k'ao-shih chih-tu shih* (A history of the Chinese civil service examination system), pp. 299–306.

12. The memorial is in *Kuang-hsü cheng-yao*, 13.18b–20; a fairly accurate English translation of the memorial is in R. S. Gundry, *China Present and Past*, pp. 387–393.

13. The joint memorial of 1905 and the imperial decree announcing the termination of the system are translated by John C. Ferguson, "The abolition of the competitive examinations in China," *Journal of the American Oriental Society*, 27: 79–87 (1906).

14. From *Kuang-hsü cheng-yao*, 29.7–9.

15. Tai Hung-tz'u and Tuan-fang, *Ou-Mei cheng-chih yao-i*, 4, sec. 1, 30–33b.

16. *Ibid.*, 2b–5.

17. We will not attempt here any judgment of Yuan's career; two American scholars have dealt with different aspects of it in dissertations. (See last two entries under Sources.)

CHAPTER XXI. ECONOMIC DEVELOPMENT

Sources

The main sources for Sheng Hsuan-huai and Chang Chien are the *Yü-chai ts'un-kao* and *Chang Chi-tzu chiu-lu*, respectively. Both contain full collections of their writings well arranged and printed. In addition to the short biography at the beginning of each of these works, there is a detailed biography of Chang Chien by his son, containing many quotations from his writings; and Chiang I-hsueh, "Chang Chien i-chuan," is a draft biography intended for a "dynastic" history of the period of the Republic. Apart from these, P'eng Tse-i's "Chang Chien ti ssu-hsiang chi ch'i shih-yeh" (Chang's ideas and career) is a good summary based on *Chang Chi-tzu chiu-lu*. There is an English pamphlet entitled *Life of the Honourable Chang Chien with an Account of the Enterprises Inaugurated by Him* (Shanghai, 1915), author's name unknown; and there are two short papers by Davy H. McCall, "Chang Chien and the Establishment of the Tung-chow Mills," and "Chang Chien — Mandarin turned Manufacturer."

For other industrialists we may mention Hsü Jun (1838–1911), *Hsü Yü-chai tzu-hsü nien-p'u*, the informative autobiography of an important business man, which contains many references to the enterprises of others of his wide acquaintance; Mu Hsiang-yueh (1877–1943), *Ou-ch'u ssu-shih tzu-shu*, the reminiscences of a leading textile manufacturer, written to mark his fortieth birthday, and published in 1926; and Hsü Ying's *Tang-tai Chung-kuo shih-yeh jen-wu chih*, a sketch of twenty-eight contemporary industrialists based on interviews and useful for general reference. Yang Lien-sheng's *Topics in Chinese History*, containing carefully selected sources under each topic, is an important tool for students in Chinese history and economics. The same author's *Money and Credit in China* is a critical and compact account which supplies useful background material regarding economic development.

While this is not the place for a list of works on Chinese economic growth in this period, the following works are noteworthy for our purpose: Frank M. Tamagna, *Banking and Finance in China*; Li P'ei-en, "Chin-pai-nien lai Chung-kuo chih yin-hang" (Banking in China during the last century); *Yin-hang nien-chien* (Yearbook of banking); "Modern Business in China: the Bank of China before 1935" by S. H. Chafkin; "Ch'ing-mo Han-yang t'ieh-ch'ang" (The Hanyang iron and steel works 1890–1908) by Ch'üan Han-sheng; the *Rise of the Modern Chinese Business Class* by Marion J. Levy, Jr. and Shih Kuo-heng; *Eastern Industrialization and its Effect on the West* by G .E. Hubbard; and Hsia Yen-te, *Chung-kuo chin-pai-nien ching-chi ssu-hsiang*, on economic thought. The last, by Hsia, is a very useful selection of excerpts from many of the men studied in the present volume, with sources and notes.

Notes

1. H. B. Morse, *The International Relations of the Chinese Empire*, III, 46.
2. See *Ta-Ch'ing Kuang-hsü hsin fa-ling* (New laws and ordinances of the Kuang-hsü reign), compiled by the Commercial Press, Shanghai, 1909, ts'e 16, section 10.
3. Kung Chün, *Chung-kuo hsin-kung-yeh fa-chan shih ta-kang*, pp. 65–88.
4. Cp. Weng Wen-hao, "Wu-shih-nien lai ti ching-chi chien-she" (Economic reconstruction in the last fifty years) in *Wu-shih-nien lai ti Chung-kuo* (China during the last fifty years), p. 98.
5. *Ibid.*, pp. 98–99; and Tamagna, *Banking and Finance in China*, p. 37.
6. Hsi-yin, "Keng-tzu ch'üan-huo tung-nan hu-pao chih chi-shih" (A reliable account of the protection [of foreigners and Chinese] in southeastern China during the Boxer Uprising), *Jen-wen*, 2.7: 1–7 (September 1931).
7. J. O. P. Bland, *Li Hung-chang*, p. 121.
8. H. B. Morse, *The International Relations*, III, 362.
9. *Yü-chai ts'un-kao*, 24.27b.
10. *Ibid.*, 31.32b–33.
11. *Ibid.*, 1.14–15.
12. Cp. *ibid.*, 25.12b.
13. See Sheng Hsuan-huai's biography, *hsing-shu*, in *Yü-chai ts'un-kao*, ts'e 1.61.
14. Cp. Chang Hsiao-jo, *Nan-t'ung Chang Chi-chih hsien-sheng chuan-chi* (A biography of Chang Chien), pp. 67–8; 228–29.
15. From Chang Chien, *Chang Chi-tzu chiu-lu, shih-yeh-lu*, 1.7b–8.
16. Cp. *ibid.*, 6.5b–6.
17. *Ibid.*, 8.33b–36.
18. From *Chang Chi-tzu chiu-lu, chuan-lu*, 4.1–34.
19. See Chang Chien's chronological biography at the beginning of *Chang Chi-tzu chiu-lu*.
20. *Nan-t'ung Chang Chi-chih hsien-sheng chuan-chi*, p. 5.

21. From *Chang Chi-tzu chiu-lu, shih-yeh lu,* 5.13b–14.
22. *Ibid., cheng-wen lu,* 9.3b–5b.

CHAPTER XXII. LIANG CH'I-CH'AO AND NATIONALISM

SOURCES

For sources on Liang, see under Chapter XVI.

NOTE

1. From *Hsin-min ts'ung-pao,* 1: 1–10 (January 1902).

CHAPTER XXIII. SUN YAT-SEN'S EARLY REVOLUTIONARY PROGRAM

SOURCES

For sources on Sun Yat-sen see Chapter XXVII below.

NOTES

1. Sun Yat-sen's letter to Li Hung-chang is in Tsou Lu, *Chung-kuo Kuo-min-tang shih-kao* (Draft history of the Kuomintang of China), Min-chih shu-chü edition, 1.6–19. A Japanese translation of Sun's letter is in Kayano Chōchi, *Chūka-minkoku kakumei hikyu,* and an extract appears in Léon Wieger, *Chine moderne,* vol. 1.

2. The Manifesto of the Hsing-Chung-hui is in *Chung-shan ch'üan-shu,* section on manifestoes, 4.1–4, and in Tsou Lu, *Chung-kuo Kuo-min-tang shih-kao,* pt. 1.2–6, with introductory note and complete text. An English excerpt from the Manifesto is in Lyon Sharman, *Sun Yat-sen, his Life and its Meaning: A Critical Biography,* p. 36, and the excerpt is quoted in full by Donald G. Tewksbury, *Source Book on Far Eastern Political Ideologies, Modern Period, China-Japan,* p. 1.

3. From *Chung-shan ch'üan-shu,* "Manifestoes," 4.1–4. See also Tsou Lu, *Chung-kuo Kuo-min-tang shih-kao,* 1.2.

4. T'ien-yun (lit., "Heavenly rotation") was the reign title used by Chang Pu-wei at the end of the Ming Dynasty (1637). It was repeatedly used in the documents issued by the T'ung-meng-hui, indicating the revolutionists' repudiation of Manchu rule by their refusal to adopt its reign style.

5. Shih Ching-t'ang (posthumous name, Chin Kao-tsu) was the founder of the Chin Dynasty (936–947). He was a traitor towards the later T'ang and was made emperor by the Khitans. See *Chiu Wu-tai shih* (The old history of the Five Dynasties), *chüan* 75–76. For Wu San-kuei, see Hummel, pp. 877–80.

6. This slogan and the three preceding are about all of this document that has heretofore been available in English. See Donald G. Tewksbury, *Source Book on Far Eastern Political Ideologies, Modern Period,* p. 7.

CHAPTER XXIV. THE SEARCH FOR NEW PRINCIPLES

SOURCES

a. *The Variety of the New Thought*

The following items are suggested in addition to the bibliography given in Wen-han Kiang (Chiang Wen-han), *The Chinese Student Movement,* pp. 173–176, which deals principally with the period after 1923; for source materials, see also Fairbank and Liu, *Modern China,* especially section 8, "Intellectual and Literary History." For a general introduction, Ts'ai Yuan-p'ei, "Wu-shih-nien-lai Chung-kuo chih che-hsueh" (Chinese philosophy in the last fifty years), is noteworthy. Note also Wu Ch'i-yuan, *Chung-kuo hsin-wen-hua yun-tung kai-kuan* (A general review of China's new culture movement); Ch'en Tuan-chih, *Wu-ssu yun-tung chih shih ti p'ing-chia* (A historical review of the May Fourth Movement); Hua Kang, *Wu-ssu yun-tung shih* (A history of the May Fourth Movement); Liu Hsi-san, "Wu-ssu i-hou Chung-kuo ko-p'ai ssu-hsiang-chia tui-yü Hsi-yang wen-ming ti t'ai-tu" (Attitudes of Chinese thinkers of various groups toward Western civilization since the May Fourth Movement), which gives an all-round summary of all schools of thought; Huang Ti, "Wu-ssu i-lai chih Chung-kuo hsueh-ch'ao" (Chinese student strikes since the May Fourth Movement), which was a master's thesis in sociology. Ch'en Jen-pai, "Lun wu-ssu yun-tung chih hua-shih-tai ti i-i" (On the significance of the epoch-making May Fourth Movement), and Hu Shih, "Wo-men tui-yü Hsi-yang chin-tai wen-ming ti t'ai-tu" (Our attitude toward modern Western civilization), are two useful magazine articles. Wang Tsao-shih, "Chung Hsi chieh-ch'u hou she-hui-shang ti pien-hua" (Social changes after the contact between China and the West), traces developments after the Opium War. The *Shen-pao* volume, *Tsui-chin chih wu-shih-nien*, and P'an Kung-chan, *Wu-shih-nien-lai ti Chung-kuo* (China in the last fifty years), both have valuable entries.

About Ku Hung-ming, besides his own writings both in Chinese and Western languages, there are essays by Lin Yü-t'ang, Yuan Chen-ying, Ssu-luan, Meng Ch'i, Ch'en Ch'ang-hua, Chen Ying, and others in the magazine *Jen-chien shih*, and an article by Hu Shih in *Ta-kung-pao*, literary supplement, no. 164. Chang Shih-chao, *Ch'ang-sha Chang-shih ts'ung-kao* (Collected drafts of Chang Shih-chao of Changsha), is an interesting source. On nationalism, see *Kuo-chia chu-i chiang-yen chi* (Collected essays on nationalism). On Chang Ping-lin, see Hsü Shou-ch'ang's volume by that title. T'ai-hsü, *Jen-sheng kuan ti k'o-hsueh* (A science of the philosophy of life), is a discussion of Chinese cultural problems from a Buddhist point of view. See also Wu Ching-heng, *Wu Chih-hui hsien-sheng wen-ts'un* (Collected essays of Wu Chih-hui); and Li Shih-ch'en, *Jen-sheng che-hsueh* (Philosophy of life). Other helpful items for this period include Chang Chien-fu, "Chin san-pai-nien Chung-kuo min-tsu ko-ming yun-tung ti yen-chin" (The development of the Chinese nationalist revolution during the last three hundred years); Kuo Chan-po, *Chin wu-shih-nien Chung-kuo ssu-hsiang shih* (A history of Chinese thought during the last fifty years); Ch'en Hsü-ching, *Chung-kuo wen-hua ti ch'u-lu* (The future of Chinese culture); and Yang K'un, "Chung-kuo tsui-chin san-shih-nien chih ch'u-pan chieh" (Chinese publications during the last thirty years [mainly books on sociology]).

b. *Ts'ai Yuan-p'ei and Freedom of Education*

The main educational ideas of Ts'ai Yuan-p'ei are preserved in his collected speeches, articles, and letters published under the title, *Ts'ai Chieh-min hsien-sheng yen-hsing lu*. A succinct autobiography, "Wo tsai chiao-yü-chieh ti ching-yen," is in *Tzu-chuan chih i-chang*, edited by T'ao K'ang-te; and a short biography entitled *Ts'ai Chieh-min hsien-sheng chuan-lueh* was written by Kao Nai-t'ung. Ts'ai's connection with Peking University is described by himself in "Wo tsai Pei-ching ta-hsueh ti ching-kuo" and in another article, "Ts'ai Yuan-p'ei yü Pei-ching ta-hsueh," written by Lao Kan. See also Ts'ai Yuan-p'ei, "The Development of Chinese Education," in *Asiatic Review*. There is a special memorial issue, "Chui-tao Ts'ai Chieh-min hsien-sheng t'e-chi," in *Tung-fang tsa-chih*; another in *Yü-chou feng*, 24 and 28; and two memorial volumes, *Ch'ing-chu Ts'ai Yuan-p'ei hsien-sheng liu-shih-wu-sui lun-wen chi*, presented to him by fellows and assistants of the Academia Sinica and published in 1933. These volumes contain academic articles, but the brief preface notes Dr. Ts'ai's contribution to the academic world through his directorship of the Academia Sinica. Chou Tso-jen's "Chi Ts'ai Chieh-min hsien-sheng ti shih" is an interesting short essay. Miss Chin-hsieo Tai has written a doctoral dissertation in the Harvard Graduate School of Education on "The Life and Work of Ts'ai Yuan-p'ei," with extensive bibliography.

NOTES

1. See the volume by Conrad Brandt, Benjamin Schwartz, and John K. Fairbank, *A Documentary History of Chinese Communism*, which deals with the development of Marxist-Leninist doctrine in China from 1921 to 1950.

2. For more biographical information, see *Who's Who in China*, 1926 and 1936 editions.

3. See Robert K. Sakai, "Ts'ai Yuan-p'ei as a Synthesizer of Western and Chinese Thought," *Papers on China*, Cambridge, 3: 170–192 (May 1949). Mr. Sakai has written a doctoral dissertation at Harvard on "Politics and Education in Modern China."

4. T'ang Leang-li, *The Foundations of Modern China*, p. 87. See also Ts'ai Yuan-p'ei, "Wo tsai Pei-ching ta-hsueh ti ching-kuo."

5. From *Ts'ai Chieh-min hsien-sheng yen-hsing lu*, pp. 189–203.

6. Ch. 9 of the *Book of Rites* (*Li chi*): "Ta-tao chih hsing yeh, t'ien-hsia wei kung" ("When the great doctrine is carried out, the empire will be for the common weal"). This sentence is condensed by Ts'ai as "Ta-tao wei kung."

7. From *Ts'ai Chieh-min hsien-sheng yen-hsing lu*, pp. 314–325.

8. *Ibid.*, p. 227.

CHAPTER XXV. EARLY CONVERTS TO MARXISM

SOURCES

The primary sources on Ch'en Tu-hsiu are the *Tu-hsiu wen-ts'un*, *Hsin-ch'ing-nien*, vol. 1, and a short autobiography about his early life, "Shih-an tzu-chuan." See also the old periodicals *Hsiang-tao* and *Mei-chou p'ing-lun*; Ch'en Tung-hsiao (comp.), *Ch'en*

Tu-hsiu p'ing-lun (A critique of Ch'en Tu-hsiu); B. Schwartz, "Ch'en Tu-hsiu, his Pre-Communist Phase," *Papers on China*, 2.167–197, and his *Chinese Communism and the Rise of Mao.* There are also several entries referring to Ch'en Tu-hsiu in C. Martin Wilbur (ed.), *Chinese Sources on the History of the Chinese Communist Movement.* A booklet, *Ch'en Tu-hsiu ti tsui-hou chien-chieh* (Ch'en Tu-hsiu's final views), was published by the Tzu-yu Chung-kuo ch'u-pan she in Hongkong (1950), and has been translated for publication in English.

On Li Ta-chao see *Hsin-ch'ing-nien*, vols. 1–7, and *Hsiang-tao* and other magazines listed in *Chung-kuo hsin-wen-hsueh ta-hsi*, vol. 10, compiled by A-ying. Li also wrote a book on democracy, *P'ing-min chu-i.* Chin Yü-min, "Li Ta-chao yü wu-ssu yun-tung" (Li Ta-chao and the May Fourth Movement), in *Kuan-ch'a*, 6.13 (May 1, 1950), and Yang Yung-kuo, "Li Shou-ch'ang hsien-sheng ti ssu-hsiang" (The thought of Li Shou-ch'ang [Ta-chao]), *Tu-shu yü ch'u-pan*, no. 2: 4–7 (1947), are short articles of some use. See also Hua Ying-shen, *Chung-kuo Kung-ch'an-tang lieh-shih chuan*, in which there is a short biography of Li Ta-chao.

For selections from the works on Chinese communism published in Japanese, see the two bibliographies in Brandt, Schwartz, and Fairbank, *A Documentary History of Chinese Communism*; and Ichiro Shirato (C. M. Wilbur, ed.), *Japanese Sources on the History of the Chinese Communist Movement* (New York: East Asian Institute of Columbia University, 1953), 69 pp.

NOTES

1. "Ching-kao ch'ing-nien" (*Ching-kao*, lit., respectful warning), first article in the first issue, *Hsin-ch'ing-nien*, 1.1 (Sept. 15, 1915).
2. According to legend, Ts'ao-fu and Hsü Yu both refused to accept the throne when the Emperor Yao offered it to them successively, thus showing their utter contempt for worldly glory.
3. Li Ta-chao, "Wo-ti Ma-k'o-ssu chu-i kuan" (My view of Marxism), *Hsin-ch'ing-nien*, 6.5: 521–537 (May 1919).
4. "Bolshevism ti sheng-li," *Hsin-ch'ing-nien*, 5.5: 442–448 (Nov. 15, 1918).
5. *Ibid.* This and the two following quotations are presented without reference data in the Chinese text, so our retranslations have not been compared with the English originals.
6. "Preface" to *K'o-hsueh yü jen-sheng-kuan* (Science and the philosophy of life), a collection of essays edited by Ya-tung t'u-shu-kuan, pp. 5–11.

CHAPTER XXVI. HU SHIH AND PRAGMATISM IN CHINA

SOURCES

Dr. Hu has been a prolific writer during much of his career. For the chief collections of his works, see Fairbank and Liu, *Modern China*, and also the index to that volume. His *Ssu-shih tzu-shu* (Autobiography at forty) and *Hu Shih liu-hsueh jih-chi* (Hu Shih's diary when he studied abroad), which is better than his *Ts'ang-hui-shih cha-chi* (Diary of student days in America), offer much biographical material. *Hu Shih wen-ts'un* (collected essays), *Hu Shih wen-ts'un erh-chi* (second collection), and *Hu Shih wen-ts'un san-chi* (third collection) are particularly useful because they include not only his own work but also, in cases of controversy, the writings of others who discussed problems with him. His edition of the first volume of the *Chung-kuo hsin-wen-hsueh ta-hsi* contains discussions on the theory of the new literature; and his own book, *The Chinese Renaissance*, gives a remarkable summary of the Chinese cultural heritage and the new literature movement. Of works from other points of view there are: Yeh Ch'ing, *Hu Shih p'i-p'an* (Critique of Hu Shih); Wang Feng-yuan, *Chung-kuo hsin-wen-hsueh yun-tung shu-p'ing* (Narration of and comments on the new literature movement in China); and a number of articles attacking or defending his point of view, which we do not attempt to list. Note the recent volume by John De Francis, *Nationalism and Language Reform in China.*

NOTES

1. From *Hu Shih wen-ts'un* (Collected essays of Hu Shih), 4.151–164.
2. Part X of the essay, "Chinese literature in the past fifty years," in *Hu Shih wen-ts'un erh-chi* (Second collection of the essays of Hu Shih), 2.188–213. This essay was first published in *Tsui-chin chih wu-shih-nien.*

CHAPTER XXVII. SUN YAT-SEN'S REORIENTATION OF THE REVOLUTION

SOURCES

For materials in Chinese, largely unavailable in English, on Sun's career and thought, see Fairbank and Liu, *Modern China*, index. For the various changes in Sun Yat-sen's approach to the solution of China's problems, the most useful source is Hu Han-min (ed.), *Tsung-li ch'üan-chi* (Complete collection of the works of the Director-general); see also Tsou Lu, *Chung-kuo Kuo-min-tang shih-kao* (A draft history of the Kuomintang), the best work thus far available. Chou Fu-hai, *San-min chu-i chih li-lun ti t'i-hsi*, was considered one of the best textbooks of party doctrine. Lou T'ung-sun, *San-min chu-i yen-chiu*, is another textbook on the subject for beginners; while Ch'en Po-ta, *Lun Sun Chung-shan chu-i*, is a rather polite criticism and interpretation by a communist publicist. A useful book on Sun's system of thinking is Liu Ping-li, *Kuo-fu ssu-hsiang t'i-hsi*. Articles about Sun Yat-sen are numerous. In English, apart from translations of Sun's works, mention should be made of Paul M. A. Linebarger, *The Political Doctrines of Sun Yat-sen*, and Ch'ien Tuan-sheng, *The Government and Politics of China*. In Japanese, Ono Noriaki's *Son Bun*, with a short bibliography of Japanese works, may be mentioned. A recent and provocative study of the Three Principles from the point of view of Chinese philosophy may be found in Ojima Sukema, *Chūgoku no kakumei shisō*. For other works in Japanese, see Fairbank and Banno, *Japanese Studies of Modern China*. Among the numerous biographies in Western languages, that by Lyon Sharman is still one of the most reliable. A recent Western study which makes interesting use of Japanese sources is by Marius B. Jansen, *Adventurers and Revolutionaries: The Japanese and Sun Yat-sen* (Cambridge: Harvard University Press, 1954). At the headquarters of the Kuomintang Central Reform Committee in Taipei, Taiwan, valuable scholarly work is being done by Ts'ui Shu-ch'in (on the political thought of Sun Yat-sen) and by Chang Ch'i-yun (see his *Tang-shih kai-yao, chin liu-shih-nien Chung-kuo ko-ming shih* [A general history of the Kuomintang, a history of the Chinese revolution in the last sixty years], published by the Central Reform Committee [Chung-yang kai-tsao wei-yuan-hui], 1952, 5 vols., 2724 pp.).

NOTES

1. See Tsou Lu, *Chung-kuo Kuo-min-tang, shih-kao*, pp. 159–170, and William E. Nelson, "One-party Government in China: its Origins in the Revolutionary Movement," in *Papers on China*, vol. 2.

2. From "Neng-chih pi neng-hsing," ch. 6 of *Sun Wen hsueh-shuo* (The philosophy of Sun Yat-sen), in *Chung-shan ch'üan-shu*, 4.50–63.

3. From a speech delivered to Kuomintang members during the reorganization of the Kuomintang, December 1, 1923, *Tsung-li ch'üan-chi*, 2.314–324. Sentences from this speech are also translated in Tsui Shu-chin, "The Influence of the Canton-Moscow Entente," p. 102.

4. *Hsun-lien yuan*: officially Borodin held the position of adviser to the Nationalist Government.

CHAPTER XXVIII. LIANG CH'I-CH'AO'S REVIEW OF CHINA'S PROGRESS, 1873–1922

SOURCES

For sources on Liang, see under Ch. XVI. For a recent list of works on the Republican period, see Su Te-yung, "Min-kuo shih-liao shu-mu ch'u-pien" (A bibliography of the history of the Republic of China), *Hsueh-shu chi-k'an*, 1.3:220–227 (March 1953), 1.4:152–176 (June), 2.1:160–181 (September), published by Chung-hua wen-hua ch'u-pan shih-yeh wei-yuan-hui, Taiwan.

NOTES

1. Liang Ch'i-ch'ao, "Lao-tzu che-hsueh" (The philosophy of Lao-tzu), *Yin-ping-shih ho-chi, Wen-chi* (Collected essays), pt. 63: 14–14b (1920).

2. "Tung-nan ta-hsueh k'o-pi kao-pieh tz'u" (Parting speech after completing classes at Tung-nan University), *ibid.*, pt. 70: 3b–4 (1923).

3. From "Wu-shih-nien Chung-kuo chin-hua kai-lun," *ibid., ts'e* 14, 39.39–48.

BIBLIOGRAPHY

BIBLIOGRAPHY

This is a single alphabetic list of all items cited above, except that some Chinese titles cited in the text but not used by us are listed in the Glossary below. In some cases, complete information is unavailable; in others, the translation of titles is impossible. The quality of the items we have cited varies widely, from magistral monographs to thin brief notices, but having seen the latter we have thought it useful to include them, in the effort to save others the experience of hope and disillusionment that comes from "discovering" an article which has an interesting title but which at the end of a few pages leaves the reader exactly where he was before. This bibliography makes no effort at completeness, but our Notes and Sources have tried to indicate the jumping-off places for further research. Abbreviations (like CSPSR) which we have used above are also in this list. (A few recent items are cited only under Sources above.)

Analects of Confucius, see Waley.

A-ying 阿英 (Pen-name of Ch'ien Hsing-ts'un 錢杏邨), Chung-kuo hsin-wen-hsueh ta-hsi, vol. 10, Shih-liao, so-yin 中國新文學大系，史料，索引 (A corpus of China's new literature, historical data and index; Shanghai: Liang-yu Co., 1936), 513+100 pp. See also Chao Chia-pi.

Bain, Chester A., "Commodore Matthew Perry, Humphrey Marshall, and the Taiping Rebellion," Far Eastern Quarterly, 10.3: 258-270 (May 1951).

Bales, W. L., Tso Tsung-t'ang: Soldier and Statesman of Old China (Shanghai: Kelly and Walsh, 1937), 436 pp.

Banno Masataka 坂野正高, "Gaikō kōshō ni okeru Shimmatsu kanjin no kōdō yōshiki" 外交交涉に於ける清末官人の行動樣式 ("Behaviours of Mandarins as diplomats late in the Ch'ing Dynasty"), Kokusaihō gaikō zasshi 國際法外交雜誌, 48.4: 18-56 (October 1949), 48.6: 37-71 (December 1949).

Banno Masataka 坂野正高, "'Sō-ri ga-mon' setsuritsu no haikei" 總理衙門設立の背景 (The background of the establishment of the Tsungli Yamen), Kokusaihō gaikō zasshi 國際法外交雜誌, 51.4: 360-402 (August 1952), 51.5: 506-541 (October 1952), 52.3: 89-111 (June 1953).

Bernard, Henri, S.J., Aux Portes de la Chine; les missionnaires du seizième siècle, 1514-1588 (Tientsin: en vente à la Procure de la Mission de Sienshien, 1933), 283 pp.

Bernard, Henri, S.J., Matteo Ricci's Scientific Contribution to China, tr. by Edward Chalmers Werner (Peiping: H. Vetch, 1935), 108 pp.

Bernard, Henri, "Notes on the Introduction of the Natural Sciences," Yenching Journal of Social Studies 3: 220-241 (1941).

Bernard, Henri, S.J., "Les adaptations chinoises d'ouvrages européens: bibliographie chronologique depuis la venue des Portugais à Canton jusqu'à la mission française de Pekin, 1514-1688," Monumenta Serica 10: 1-57, 309-388 (1945).

Biggerstaff, Knight, "The Tung Wen Kuan," CSPSR 18.3: 307-340 (October 1934).

Biggerstaff, Knight, "The Ch'ung-hou Mission to France, 1870-1871," Nankai Social and Economic Quarterly, 8.3: 633-647 (October 1935).

Biggerstaff, Knight, "The Establishment of Permanent Chinese Diplomatic Missions Abroad," CSPSR 20.1: 1-41 (April 1936).

Biggerstaff, Knight, "The Official Chinese Attitude toward the Burlingame Mission," American Historical Review, 41.4: 682-702 (July 1936).

Biggerstaff, Knight, "The First Chinese Mission of Investigation sent to Europe," Pacific Historical Review, 6.4: 307-320 (December 1937).

Biggerstaff, Knight, "Anson Burlingame's Instructions from the Chinese Foreign Office," <u>Far Eastern Quarterly</u>, 1.3: 277-79 (May 1942).

Biggerstaff, Knight, "The secret correspondence of 1867-1868: views of leading Chinese statesmen regarding the further opening of China to Western influence," <u>Journal of Modern History</u>, 22.2: 122-136 (June 1950).

Bland, J.O.P., <u>Li Hung-chang</u> (New York, 1917), 327 pp.

Bland, J.O.P. and Backhouse, E., <u>China Under the Empress Dowager</u> (London, 1910), 525 pp.

Boardman, Eugene P., "Christian Influence upon the Ideology of the Taiping Rebellion," <u>Far Eastern Quarterly</u>, 10.2: 115-124 (February 1951).

Boardman, Eugene P., <u>Christian Influence upon the Ideology of the Taiping Rebellion 1851-1864</u> (The University of Wisconsin Press, 1952), 188 pp.

Bodde, Derk, <u>see</u> Feng Yu-lan.

<u>Book of Changes</u>, see Chou-i cheng-i.

<u>Book of History</u>, see Shang-shu cheng-i.

<u>Book of Rites</u>, <u>see</u> Li Ki .

Brandt, Conrad, Benjamin Schwartz, and John K. Fairbank, <u>A Documentary History of Chinese Communism</u> (Cambridge: Harvard University Press, 1952), 552 pp. (London: Allen and Unwin).

British Parliamentary Papers, <u>Correspondence relative to the Earl of Elgin's Special Mission to China and Japan 1857-1859</u>, presented to the House of Lords by command, 1859.

Britton, Roswell S., <u>The Chinese Periodical Press 1800-1912</u> (Shanghai: Kelly and Walsh, 1933), 143 pp.

Burt, E.W., "The Centenary of Timothy Richard," <u>Baptist Quarterly</u>, 343-348 (Jan.-Apr. 1945).

Burt, E.W., "Timothy Richard: his contribution to modern China," <u>International Review of Missions</u>, 293-300 (July 1945).

Cameron, Meribeth E., "The Public Career of Chang Chih-tung 1837-1909," <u>Pacific Historical Review</u>, 7.3: 187-210 (September 1938).

Cameron, Meribeth E., <u>The Reform Movement in China, 1898-1912</u> (London: Oxford University Press, 1931 edition), 223 pp.

Candler, W. A., <u>Young J. Allen</u> (Nashville: Cokesbury Press, 1931), 245 pp.

Carlson, Ellsworth, "The K'ai-p'ing Mines, 1877-1912: A Case Study of Early Chinese Industrialization" (Cambridge, Mass: dissertation for the Ph. D. in History, Harvard University, 1952).

Chafkin, S. H., "Modern business in China: The Bank of China before 1935," <u>Papers on China</u>, 2: 103-133 (May 1948).

Ch'an-an 懺庵 , "Chang P'ei-lun yü Li Hung-chang" 張佩綸與李鴻章 (Chang P'ei-lun and Li Hung-chang), <u>Ku-chin</u> 古今 , no. 50: 18-20 (July 1944).

Chang Ch'i-yun 張其昀, "Liang Jen-kung ssu-hsiang pieh-lu" 梁任公思想別錄 (Supplementary record on the ideas of Liang Ch'i-ch'ao), in <u>Ssu-hsiang yü shih-tai</u> 思想與時代, vol. 4.

Chang Chien 張謇 , <u>Chang Chi-tzu chiu-lu</u> 張李子九錄 (Collected writings of Chang Chien; Shanghai: Chung-hua shu-chü, 1931), 80+10 <u>chüan</u>.

Chang Chien 張謇, Cheng-wen lu 政聞録 (Notes on government), in Chang Chi-tzu chiu-lu.

Chang Chien 張謇, Chuan-lu 專録 (Special notes), in Chang Chi-tzu chiu-lu.

Chang Chien 張謇, Shih-yeh lu 實業録 (Notes on industry), in Chang Chi-tzu chiu-lu.

Chang Chien, Life of the Honorable Chang Chien with an Account of the Enterprizes Inaugurated by Him (Shanghai, 1915), 35 pp.

Chang Chien, see P'eng Tse-i.

Chang Chien-fu 張健甫, "Chin san-pai-nien Chung-kuo min-tsu ko-ming yun-tung ti yen-chin" 近三百年中國民族革命運動的演進 (The development of the Chinese national revolution during the last three hundred years), Chien-she yen-chiu 建設研究, 7.1: 41-47 (March 1942).

Chang Chih-tung 張之洞, Chang Wen-hsiang-kung ch'üan-chi 張文襄公全集 (The complete works of Chang Chih-tung), printed in 1928, 229 chüan.

Chang Chih-tung 張之洞, Chang Wen-hsiang-kung nien-p'u 張文襄公年譜 (A chronological biography of Chang Chih-tung), compiled by Hsü T'ung-hsin 許同莘 (Chungking: Commercial Press, 1944) 229 pp. See also Hu Chün.

Chang Chih-tung 張之洞, Chang Wen-hsiang-kung tsou-i 張文襄公奏議 (The memorials of Chang Chih-tung), in Chang Wen-hsiang-kung ch'üan-chi.

Chang Chih-tung 張之洞 "Cheng-ch'üan" 正權 (Rectification of political rights), in Chang Wen-hsiang-kung ch'üan-chi, chüan 202.

Chang Chih-tung 張之洞, "Ch'ü-tu" 去毒 (To remove the poison), in Chang Wen-hsiang-kung ch'üan-chi, chüan 202.

Chang Chih-tung 張之洞, Ch'üan-hsueh-p'ien 勸學篇 (Exhortation to study), printed in 1898, 2 chüan, in Chang Wen-hsiang-kung ch'üan-chi, chüan 202-203; see also the punctuated edition in Chien-hsi ts'un-she ts'ung-k'o 漸西村舍叢刻, and the separate edition reprinted in Chekiang in 1898.

Chang Chih-tung 張之洞, "Fei kung-chiao" 非攻教 (Condemnation of attacks on missionaries), in Chang Wen-hsiang-kung ch'üan-chi, chüan 203.

Chang Chih-tung 張之洞 "Hsün-hsü" 循序 (Following the proper order), in Chang Wen-hsiang-kung ch'üan-chi, chüan 202.

Chang Chih-tung 張之洞, "Pien-fa" 變法 (On reform), in Chang Wen-hsiang-kung ch'üan-chi, chüan 203.

Chang Chih-tung 張之洞, Shu-mu ta-wen 書目答問 (Annotated bibliography of basic Chinese works), printed in 1878, 4 chüan.

Chang Chih-tung, see also Chang Wen-hsiang-kung; Woodbridge; Tobar.

Chang Ch'iung-chang 張絅章, "Li Hung-chang i-shih i-shu" 李鴻章軼事一束 (Anecdotes about Li Hung-chang), Nü-shih-hsueh-yuan ch'i-k'an, 1.1 (Jan. 1933). Pages are not numbered consecutively.

Chang Ch'iung-chang 張絅章, "Tz'u-hsi t'ai-hou i-shih" 慈禧太后軼事 (Anecdotes about the Empress Dowager Tz'u-hsi), Nü-shih-hsueh-yuan ch'i-k'an, 1.2 (July 1933). Pages are not consecutively numbered.

Chang Ch'o-hsün 張焯焄, "Ch'i-shih-nien lai Chung-kuo ping-ch'i chih chih-tsao" 七十年來中國兵器之製造 (The making of military weapons in China during the last seventy years), Tung-fang tsa-chih, 32.2: 21-30 (1936).

Chang Chung-fu 張忠紱, "Tsung-li ko-kuo shih-wu ya-men chih yuan-ch'i" 總理各國事務衙門之源起 (The origin of the Tsungli Yamen), Wai-chiao yueh-pao, 3.1: 1-11 (1933).

Chang En-lung 張恩龍, "Ming-Ch'ing liang-tai lai-Hua wai-jen k'ao-lueh" 明清兩代來華外人考略 (A brief account of the foreigners who came to China during the Ming and Ch'ing dynasties), T'u-shu-kuan-hsueh chi-k'an 圖書館學季刊, 4. 3-4: 447-472 (Dec. 1930); and 5.1: 83-104 (March 1931).

Chang Hsi-t'ang 張西堂, Wang Ch'uan-shan hsueh-p'u 王船山學譜 (An academic sketch of Wang Fu-chih; Shanghai: Commercial Press, 1938), 219 pp.

Chang Hsi-t'ung, "The earliest phase of the introduction of western political science into China," Yenching Journal of Social Studies 5: 1-29 (July 1950).

Chang Hsiao-jo 張孝若, Nan-t'ung Chang Chi-chih hsien-sheng chuan-chi, fu nien-p'u nien-piao 南通張季直先生傳記，附年譜年表 (A biography of Mr. Chang Chi-chih, Chang Chien of Nantung, with an appended chronological sketch of life and events of Chang Chi-chih; Shanghai: Chung-hua shu-chü, 1930), 649 pp.

Chang Hsin-ch'eng 張心澂, Chung-kuo hsien-tai chiao-t'ung shih 中國現代交通史 (A history of communications in modern China), in Hsien-tai Chung-kuo-shih ts'ung-shu (Modern Chinese history series), Shanghai: Liang-yu, 1931, 618 pp.

Chang Hsing-lang 張星烺, Chung-Hsi chiao-t'ung shih-liao hui-pien 中西交通史料彙編 (A miscellaneous collection of historical materials on contact between China and the West; Peking, Fu-jen University, 1928), 6 vols.

Chang Hsing-lang 張星烺, Ou-hua tung-chien shih 歐化東漸史 (The spread of Western civilization to the east; Shanghai: Commercial Press, 1926).

Chang Kia-ngau, China's Struggle for Railroad Development (New York: John Day, 1943), 340 pp.

Chang P'ei-lun 張佩綸, Chien-yü chi 澗于集 (Collected memorials of Chang P'ei-lun; published by the author, 1918), 6 chüan.

Chang Po-chen 張伯楨, Nan-hai K'ang hsien-sheng chuan 南海康先生傳 (Biography of K'ang Yu-wei), in Ts'ang-hai ts'ung-shu 滄海叢書, ts'e 6.

Chang Po-ch'u 張伯初, "Shang-hai ping-kung-ch'ang chih shih-mo" 上海兵工廠之始末 (A complete account of the Shanghai Arsenal), Jen-wen, 5.5: 1-15 (June 1934).

Chang Shih-chao 章士釗, Ch'ang-sha Chang-shih ts'ung-kao 長沙章氏叢稿 (Collected drafts of Chang Shih-chao of Changsha; Shanghai, 1929), 197 pp.

Chang Te-ch'ang 張德昌, "Li Hung-chang chih wei-hsin yun-tung" 李鴻章之維新運動 (Li Hung-chang's reform movement), Ch'ing-hua chou-k'an 清華週刊, 35.2: 110-112 (1931).

Chang Te-tse 張德澤, "Chün-chi-ch'u chi ch'i tang-an" 軍機處及其檔案 (The Grand Council and its archives), Wen-hsien lun-ts'ung, 57-84 (1930).

Chang Ts'ai-t'ien 張采田, Ch'ing lieh-ch'ao hou-fei chuan-kao 清列朝后妃傳稿 (Draft biographies of empresses of all generations of the Ch'ing dynasty; movable-type edition, 1929), 2 ts'e.

Chang Tzu-mu 張自牧, Ying-hai lun 瀛海論 (A discussion of the circuit of the seas), in Hsiao-fang-hu-chai yü-ti ts'ung-ch'ao, ts'e 60.

Chang Wei-hua 張維華, "Ming-Ch'ing chien Chung-Hsi ssu-hsiang chih ch'ung-t'u yü ying-hsiang" 明清間中西思想之衝突與影响 (The ideological conflict between China and the West during the late Ming and early Ch'ing and its effect), <u>Hsueh-ssu</u>, 1.1: 19-24 (January 1942).

Chang Wei-hua 張維華, "Ming-Ch'ing chien Fo-Yeh chih cheng-pien" 明清間佛耶之爭辨 (Argument between Buddhists and Christians during the late Ming and early Ch'ing), <u>Hsueh-ssu</u>, 1.2: 12-17 (January 1942).

"Chang Wen-hsiang-kung yü chiao-yü chih kuan-hsi" 張文襄公與教育之關係 (Chang Chih-tung's relations with Chinese education), <u>Chiao-yü tsa-chih</u> 教育雜誌, 1.10: 19-23 (September 1909).

Chang Wen-hsiang-kung, <u>see</u> Chang Chih-tung.

Chang Yin-lin 張蔭麟, "Ming-Ch'ing chih-chi Hsi-hsueh shu-ju Chung-kuo k'ao-lueh" 明清之際西學輸入中國考略 (A brief study of the introduction of Western knowledge to China during the late Ming and early Ch'ing), <u>Ch'ing-hua hsueh-pao</u> 清華學報, 1.1: 38-69.

Chang Yin-lin 張蔭麟, "Po Shui-ch'uang ch'un-i" 跋水窗春囈 (Commentary on <u>Shui-ch'uang ch'un-i</u>), Kuo-wen chou-pao, 12.10: 1-4 (1935).

Chang Yü-chüan, "The provincial organs of foreign affairs in China," CSPSR 1.3: 47-70 (Oct. 1916).

Chao Chia-pi 趙家璧, ed., <u>Chung-kuo hsin-wen-hsueh ta-hsi</u> 中國新文學大系 (A corpus of China's new literature; Shanghai: Liang-yu Co., 1936), 10 vols. See A-ying.

Chao Feng-t'ien 趙豐田, "K'ang Ch'ang-su hsien-sheng nien-p'u kao" 康長素先生年譜稿 (A draft chronological sketch of the life of K'ang Yu-wei), <u>Shih-hsueh nien-pao</u>, vol. 2 (1934).

Chao Feng-t'ien 趙豐田, <u>Wan-Ch'ing wu-shih-nien ching-chi ssu-hsiang shih</u> 晚清五十年經濟思想史 (Economic thought during the last fifty years of the Ch'ing period), <u>Yen-ching hsueh-pao</u>, monograph series no. 18 (Peiping: Harvard-Yenching Institute, 1939), 320 pp.

Chao Hsing-kuo 趙興國, "Ch'üan-fei shih-liao chi-mu" 拳匪史料輯目 (A list of historical materials on the Boxer bandits), <u>Jen-wen</u>, 7.7: 1-4 (September 1936).

Chao I-ch'eng 趙意誠, "Wang T'ao k'ao-cheng" 王韜考證, (A study of Wang T'ao), <u>Hsueh-feng</u>, 6.1: 1-24 (February 1936).

Chao Tseng-hui 趙增輝, <u>Tseng Kuo-fan yen-hsing chih t'i-hsi</u> 曾國藩言行之體系 (The consistency of Tseng Kuo-fan's words and actions; Shanghai: Pei-hsin shu-chü, 1946).

Chao Wei-hsi 趙惟熙, <u>Hsi-hsueh shu-mu ta-wen</u> 西學書目答問 (Questions and answers on books on Western knowledge; Kweiyang, 1901), 1 ts'e.

Chen Ying 震瀛, "Chi Ku Hung-ming hsien-sheng" 記辜鴻銘先生 (Notes on Mr. Ku Hung-ming), <u>Jen-chien shih</u>, no. 18 (December 1934).

Chen Ying 震瀛, "Pu-chi Ku Hung-ming hsien-sheng" 補記辜鴻銘先生 (A supplementary note on Mr. Ku Hung-ming), <u>Jen-chien shih</u>, no. 28: 9-10 (May 1935).

Ch'en Ch'ang-hua 陳昌華 et al., "Wo so chih-tao ti Ku Hung-ming hsien-sheng" 我所知道的辜鴻銘先生 (Mr. Ku Hung-ming as I knew him), <u>Jen-chien shih</u>, no. 12: 45-46 (September 1934).

Ch'en Chen-kuo 陳振國, "Ch'ang-mao chuang-yuan Wang T'ao" 長毛狀元王韜 (Wang T'ao, the leading scholar among the long-haired rebels, [Taipings]), <u>I-ching</u>, no. 33: 41-45 (July 1937).

Ch'en Ch'i-t'ien, see Gideon Ch'en.

Ch'en Chih 陳熾, Yung-shu 庸書 (preface dated 1896, block-print 1897), 2 ts'e.

Ch'en Ch'iu 陳鍫, "Wu-hsü cheng-pien-shih fan pien-fa jen-wu chih cheng-chih ssu-hsiang" 戊戌政變時反變法人物之政治思想 (The political thought of anti-reformists during the time of the One Hundred Days of Reform), Yen-ching hsueh-pao, vol. 25: 59-106 (June 1939).

Ch'en Chung-i 陳忠倚, Huang-ch'ao ching-shih wen san-pien 三編, (Second supplement to the Huang-ch'ao ching-shih wen-pien; Shanghai: Shang-hai shu-chü, 1901), 80 chüan.

Ch'en Fu-kuang 陳復光, Yu Ch'ing i-lai chih Chung-E kuan-hsi 有清以來之中俄關係 (Sino-Russian relations since the Ch'ing dynasty; Yunnan University Law School Series, B1, 1947), 464 pp.

Ch'en, Gideon, Lin Tse-hsü, Pioneer Promoter of the Adoption of Western Means of Maritime Defense in China (Peiping: Yenching University Press, 1934), 65 pp.

Ch'en, Gideon, Tseng Kuo-fan, Pioneer Promoter of the Steamship in China (Peiping: Yenching University, 1935), 98 pp.

Ch'en, Gideon, Tso Tsung-t'ang, Pioneer Promoter of the Modern Dockyard and the Woolen Mill in China (Peiping: Yenching University, 1938), 91 pp.

Ch'en, Gideon, "Tso Tsung-t'ang: the Farmer of Hsiang-shang," Yenching Journal of Social Studies, 1.2: 211-225 (1939).

Ch'en Hsü-ching 陳序經, Chung-kuo wen-hua ti ch'u-lu 中國文化的出路 (The future of Chinese culture; Shanghai: Commercial Press, 1934), 145 pp.

Ch'en I-lin 陳翊林, Tsui-chin san-shih-nien Chung-kuo chiao-yü shih 最近三十年中國教育史 (History of Chinese education in the last thirty years; Shanghai: T'ai-p'ing-yang shu-tien, 1930), 380 pp.

Ch'en Jen-pai 陳人白, "Lun wu-ssu yun-tung chih hua-shih-tai ti i-i" 論五四運動之劃時代的意義 (On the significance of the epoch-making May Fourth Movement), Ch'iu-chen tsa-chih 求真雜誌, 1.1: 6-17 (May 1946).

Ch'en, Kenneth, "Matteo Ricci's contribution to and influence on geographical knowledge in China," Journal of the American Oriental Society 59: 325-359, 509 (1939).

Ch'en Kung-lu 陳恭祿, "Chia-wu-luan hou keng-tzu-luan ch'ien Chung-kuo pien-fa yun-tung chih yen-chiu" 甲午亂後庚子亂前中國變法運動之研究 (A study of the reform movement after 1895 and before 1900), Wen-che chi-k'an 文哲, 3.1: 57-127 (1933).

Ch'en Kung-lu 陳恭祿, Chung-kuo chin-tai shih 中國近代史 (Modern Chinese history; Shanghai: Commercial Press, 1938), 860 pp.

Ch'en Kung-lu 陳恭祿, "Tseng Kuo-fan yü hai-chün" 曾國藩與海軍 (Tseng Kuo-fan and the navy), Wen-che chi-k'an, 3.4: 691-728 (1934).

Ch'en Lu 陳陸 "Ya-p'ien-chan yü Chung-kuo chün-ch'i" 鴉片戰與中國軍器 (The Opium War and Chinese weapons), Chung-ho, 1.8: 76-92 (Aug. 1940).

Ch'en Lu 陳陸, "Lin Wen-chung-kung i-shu shu" 林文忠公遺書述 (Notes on Lin Tse-hsü's works), Chung-ho, 2.12: 39-52 (December 1941).

Ch'en Pang-hsien 陳邦賢, Chung-kuo i-hsueh shih 中國醫學史 (History of medicine in China; Shanghai: Commercial Press, 1937), 406 pp.

Ch'en Po-ta 陳伯達, Lun Sun Chung-shan chu-i 論孫中山主義 (On the principles of Sun Yat-sen; Shanghai: Tso-che ch'u-pan she, 1946), 164 pp.

Ch'en Shou-yi 陳受頤 , "Ming-mo Ch'ing-ch'u Yeh-su-hui-shih ti ju-chiao-kuan chi ch'i fan-ying" 明末清初耶穌會士的儒教觀及其反應 (The Jesuits' conception of Confucianism in the late Ming and early Ch'ing and its repercussions in China), Kuo-hsueh chi-k'an 國學季刊, 5.2: 1-64 (1935).

Ch'en Shou-yi, "The religious influence of early Jesuits on Emperor Ch'ung-cheng of the Ming dynasty", T'ien-hsia Monthly, 8.5: 397-419 (May 1939), and 9.1: 35-47 (August 1939).

Ch'en Teng-yuan 陳登元 , "Hsi-hsueh lai-Hua shih kuo-jen chih wu-tuan t'ai-tu" 西學來華時國人之武斷態度 (The Chinese dogmatic attitude toward Western knowledge when it was first introduced into China), Tung-fang tsa-chih, 27.8: 61-76 (April 1930).

Ch'en T'i-ch'iang 陳體强 , Chung-kuo wai-chiao hsing-cheng 中國外交行政 (Administration of China's foreign relations; Chungking: Commercial Press, 1943).

Ch'en Tu-hsiu 陳獨秀 , "Ching-kao ch'ing-nien" 敬告青年 (Call to youth), Hsin ch'ing-nien, 1.1 (Sept. 15, 1915).

Ch'en Tu-hsiu 陳獨秀 , "Shih-an tzu-chuan" 實庵自傳 (The autobiography of Ch'en Tu-hsiu), in T'ao K'ang-te, Tzu-chuan chih i-chang, pp. 13-30.

Ch'en Tu-hsiu 陳獨秀 , Tu-hsiu wen-ts'un 獨秀文存 (Collected writings of [Ch'en] Tu-hsiu), 4 vols. (Shanghai: Ya-tung Book Co., 9th ed., 1933, 1st ed. 1922).

Ch'en Tu-hsiu ,"K'o-hsueh yü jen-sheng-kuan hsü" 科學與人生觀序 (Preface to K'o-hsueh yü jen-sheng-kuan, Science and Philosophy), 2 vols. (Shanghai: Ya-tung t'u-shu-kuan, 1st ed., 1923.; 1925).

Ch'en Tu-hsiu 陳獨秀 , Ch'en Tu-hsiu ti tsui-hou chien-chieh 陳獨秀的最後見解 (Ch'en Tu-hsiu's final point of view; Hongkong: Tzu-yu Chung-kuo ch'u-pan she 1950), 54 pp.

Ch'en Tuan-chih 陳端志 , Wu-ssu yun-tung chih shih ti p'ing-chia 五四運動之史的評價 (An historical evaluation of the May Fourth Movement; Shanghai: Sheng-huo, 1935), 390 pp.

Ch'en Tung-hsiao 陳東曉 (comp.), Ch'en Tu-hsiu p'ing-lun 陳獨秀評論 (A critique of Ch'en Tu-hsiu; Peiping: Tung-ya Book Co., 1933), 256 pp.

Ch'en Wen-chin 陳文進 , "Ch'ing-tai chih tsung-li ya-men chi ch'i ching-fei" 清代之總理衙門及其經費 (The Tsungli Yamen and its expenditures during the Ch'ing dynasty), Chung-kuo chin-tai ching-chi-shih yen-chiu chi-k'an, 1.1: 49-50 (November 1932).

Ch'en Yuan 陳垣 , "Yung-Ch'ien chien feng T'ien-chu-chiao chih tsung-shih" 雍乾間奉天主教之宗室 (Members of the imperial family who worshipped Catholicism during the periods of Yung-cheng and Ch'ien-lung), Fu-jen hsueh-chih, 3.2: 1-36 (July 1932).

Ch'en Yuan 陳垣 , "T'ang Jo-wang yü Mu Ch'en-wen" 湯若望與木陳忞 (Adam Schall von Bell and Mu Ch'en-wen), Fu-jen hsueh-chih 7.1-2: 1-28 (December 1938).

Cheng Hao-sheng 鄭鶴聲 , "Pa-shih-nien lai kuan-pan pien-i shih-yeh chih chien-t'ao," 八十年來官辦編譯事業之檢討 (An examination of government directed translation work during the past eighty years), Shuo-wen yueh-k'an, 4: 493-529 (May 1944).

Cheng Kuan-ying 鄭觀應 , Sheng-shih wei-yen 盛世危言 (Warnings to the seemingly prosperous age), 6 chüan (printed in 1893, preface dated 1892).

Cheng Shih-hsü 鄭師許 "Ming-Ch'ing liang-tai ti chün-ch'i pien-ko chi ch'i ying-hsiang" 明清兩代的軍器變革及其影响 (Changes in military equipment during the Ming and Ch'ing dynasties and its effects), Hsin-Chung-hua (new series) 新中華 , 2.6: 59-70 (1944).

Ch'eng P'ei 程沛, "Ch'i-yeh-chia Chang Chi-chih" 企業家張季直 (The businessman Chang Chi-chih), Sheng-huo yü chih-shih 生活與智識, 1.7: 19-23 (1947).

Chi-ho yuan-pen 幾何原本, translation of Euclid's Elements of Geometry, first 6 chüan by Matteo Ricci and Hsü Kuang-ch'i 徐光啟 (reprint of the 1607 translation, revised and printed in final form in 1611), the following 9 chüan by Li Shan-lan 李善蘭 and Alexander Wylie (printed in 1858).

Ch'i Ssu-ho 齊思和, "Wei Yuan yü wan-Ch'ing hsueh-feng" 魏源與晚清學風 (Wei Yuan and late Ch'ing scholarship), Yen-ching hsueh-pao, no. 39: 177-226 (December 1950).

Ch'i-ying 耆英, Yueh-t'ai yü-sung 越臺與頌, 2 ts'e (Canton: Fu-wen-chai edition, 1848).

Chiang Fang-chen 蔣方震, "Chung-kuo wu-shih-nien lai chün-shih pien-ch'ien shih" 中國五十年來軍事變遷史 (A history of Chinese military development during the past fifty years), in Shen-pao-kuan, Tsui-chin chih wu-shih-nien, 1-9.

Chiang Hsing-te 蔣星德, Tseng Kuo-fan chih sheng-p'ing chi shih-yeh 曾國藩之生平及事業 (Tseng Kuo-fan's life and career; Shanghai: Commercial Press, first edition, 1935, third printing, 1936), 263 pp.

Chiang I-hsueh 蔣逸雪, "Chang Chien i-chuan," 張謇擬傳 (Draft biography of Chang Chien), Shuo-wen yueh-k'an 3.8: 101-103 (September 1942).

Chiang Kai-shek, China's Destiny and Chinese Economic Theory, with notes and commentary by Philip Jaffe (New York: Roy Publishers, 1947), 347 pp.

Chiang Monlin, Tides from the West, A Chinese Autobiography (New Haven: Yale University Press, 1947), 282 pp.

Chiang Shu-ko 姜書閣, Chung-kuo chin-tai chiao-yü chih-tu 中國近代教育制度 (Modern educational system of China; Shanghai: Commercial Press, 1934), 203 pp.

Chiang T'ing-fu, see Tsiang, T. F.

Chiang Wen-han, see Kiang, Wen-han.

Chiang Yung 江庸, "Wu-shih-nien lai Chung-kuo chih fa-chih" 五十年來中國之法制 (China's legal system in the past fifty years), in Shen-pao-kuan, Tsui-chin chih wu-shih-nien, 1-10.

Chien Po-tsan 翦伯贊 ed., I-ho t'uan 義和團 (The Boxer movement), 4 vols. (Shanghai: Shen-chou kuo-kuang-she, 1951).

Ch'ien Hsing-ts'un, see A-ying.

Ch'ien Mu 錢穆, Chung-kuo chin san-pai-nien hsueh-shu shih 中國近三百年學術史 (A history of Chinese academic thought during the last three hundred years), 2 vols. (Chungking: Commercial Press, 1945).

Ch'ien Tuan-sheng, The Government and Politics of China (Cambridge: Harvard University Press, 1950), 526 pp.

Chih Kuei 志圭, "Ch'ing-tai K'ang-Liang wei-hsin yun-tung yü ko-ming-tang chih kuan-hsi chi ying-hsiang" 清代康梁維新運動與革命黨之關係及影響 (The reform movement of K'ang and Liang in the Ch'ing dynasty, its relation to the revolutionary party and its influence), Chien-kuo yueh-k'an 建國月刊, 9.2: 1-10 (August 1933).

Ch'ih Chung-hu 池仲祜, "Hai-chün ta-shih chi" 海軍大事記 (Great events of the navy), in Tso Shun-sheng 左舜生, Chung-kuo chin-pai-nien shih tzu-liao hsü-pien 中國近百年史資料續編, 2: 323-363.

"Ch'ih-kao Ying-i shuo-t'ieh" 斥告英夷説帖 (Placard of the partiotic people of Kwangtung denouncing the English barbarians), in IWSM-TK 31:15-20.

Chin Liang 金梁, Chin-shih jen-wu chih 近世人物志 (A gazeteer of modern personages; 1934), 366 pp.

Chin Yü-min 金毓敏, "Li Ta-chao yü wu-ssu yun-tung" 李大剑與五四運動 (Li Ta-chao and the May Fourth Movement), Kuan-ch'a 觀察, 6.13 (May 1, 1950).

Ch'in Han-ts'ai 秦翰才, Tso Wen-hsiang-kung tsai hsi-pei 左文襄公在西北 (Tso Tsung-t'ang in the Northwest; Chungking: Commercial Press, 1945), 229 pp.

Chinese Repository, published in Macao and Canton, May 1832 to December 1851, monthly.

Chinese Social and Political Science Review, see CSPSR.

Ch'ing-ch'ao hsü wen-hsien t'ung-k'ao, see Liu Chin-tsao.

Ch'ing-shih kao, see CSK.

Ch'ing-shih lieh-chuan, see CSLC.

Ch'ing shih-lu, see CSL.

Chiu Wu-tai shih 舊五代史 (The old history of the Five Dynasties) in Er-shih-ssu shih (T'ung-wen shu-chü edition, 1894).

Ch'iu-tzu-ch'iang chai 求自强齋, comp., Hsi-cheng ts'ung-shu 西政叢書 (Collectanea of books on Western institutions; Shen-chi shu-chuang, 1897).

Chou Chen-fu 周振甫, "Yen Fu ssu-hsiang chuan-pien chih p'ou-hsi" 嚴復思想轉變之剖析 (An analysis of the change of Yen Fu's thought), Hsueh-lin, no. 3: 113-133 (January 1941).

Chou Chen-fu 周振甫, "Yen Fu ti Chung-Hsi wen-hua kuan" 嚴復的中西文化觀 (Yen Fu's view of Chinese and Western culture), Tung-fang tsa-chih, 34.1: 293-303 (1937).

Chou Fu-hai 周佛海, San-min chu-i chih li-lun ti t'i-hsi 三民主義之理論的體系 (The theoretical system of San-min chu-i; Shanghai: Hsin-sheng-ming yueh-k'an she, 1928), 354 pp.

Chou-i cheng-i 周易正義 (The Book of Changes), in Shih-san-ching chu-su 十三經注疏, ed. by Juan Yuan, ts'e 1-4 (1892).

Chou Tso-jen 周作人, "Chi Ts'ai Chieh-min hsien-sheng ti shih" 記蔡孑民先生的事 (Anecdotes about Ts'ai Yuan-p'ei), Ku-chin, no. 6.

Chou Tzu-ya 周子亞, "Li Hung-chang yü fan-Jih wai-chiao" 李鴻章與反日外交 (Li Hung-chang and his anti-Japan diplomacy), San-min chu-i pan-yueh k'an 三民主義半月刊, 1.9: 21-23 (1942).

Ch'ou-pan i-wu shih-mo, see IWSM.

Chu Chih-yü 朱之瑜, Shun-shui i-shu 舜水遺書 (Collected works of Chu Chih-yü), 12 ts'e (1913).

Chu Chih-yü 朱之瑜, Yang-chiu shu-lueh 陽九述略 (A brief account of the Yang-chiu [misfortune]), in Shun-shui i-shu 舜水遺書 (Collected works of Chu Chih-yü), 12 ts'e (movable type edition of 1913), see ts'e 11.

Chu I-hsin 朱一新, Wu-hsieh-t'ang ta-wen 無邪堂答問 (Answers to questions in the orthodox studio), author's preface dated 1892, ts'e 1-5, in Cho-an ts'ung-kao 拙盒叢稿, 16 ts'e (Pao-chen t'ang, 1896).

Chu K'o-ching 朱克敬 , Jou-yuan hsin-shu 柔遠新書 (A new volume on the cherishing of men from afar), 4 chüan, 4 ts'e (Shanghai, 1884).

Chu Shih-chieh 朱世傑 , Ssu-yuan yü-chien 四元玉鑑 (Precious mirror of the four elements), chüan 3, in Pai-fu-t'ang suan-hsueh ts'ung-shu 白芙堂算學叢書.

Chu Shun-shui, see Chu Chih-yǔ.

Chu Wu 竹塢, "Wo-kuo chih lu-chǔn" 我國之陸軍 (The army of our country), Kuo-feng pao 國風報, 1.21: 47-74 (1910).

Ch'u Ch'eng-po 褚成博 , Chien-cheng-t'ang che-kao 堅正堂摺稿 (Memorials of Ch'u Ch'eng-po), 2 chüan (block-print edition of 1905).

Ch'u-chin 楚金 , "Tao-kuang hsueh-shu" 道光學術 (The academic studies of the Tao-kuang period), Chung-ho, 2.1: 1-16 (Jan. 1, 1941).

Ch'u-chin 楚金 , Kuo Yun-hsien shou-cha ping-pa 郭筠仙手札並跋 (Notes on Kuo Sung-tao's autographic correspondence), Chung-ho, 1.12: 68-75 (February 1941); and Kuo Yun-hsien shou-cha tz'u-chi 次輯 (a supplementary collection), Chung-ho, 5.2: 48-51 (February 1944).

Ch'ǔ Chung-hsuan-kung, see Ch'ǔ Shih-ssu.

Ch'ǔ Hsuan-ying 瞿宣穎 , "Tu Tseng Wen-cheng-kung chi pi-chi" 讀曾文正公集筆記 (On reading Tseng Kuo-fan's collected works), Hsin-min yueh-k'an 新民月刊 , 1.2: 1-15 (1935).

Ch'ǔ Shih-ssu 瞿式耜 , Ch'ǔ Chung-hsuan-kung wen-chi 瞿忠宣公文集 (Collected essays of Ch'ǔ Shih-ssu; Kiangsu reprint edition, 1887).

Ch'ǔ Tui-chih 瞿兌之, "Keng-hsin shih-chi yao-lu" 庚辛史籍要錄 (An annotated bibliography of books on the events of 1900 and 1901), Kuo-wen chou-pao, 11.3: 1-6 (January 1934).

Ch'uan, T. K., "Tseng Kuo-fan," T'ien-hsia Monthly 2: 121-137 (February 1936).

Ch'uan Han-sheng 全漢昇, "Ch'ing-mo ti Hsi-hsueh yuan-ch'u Chung-kuo shuo" 清末的西學源出中國說 (The theory of the Chinese origin of Western sciences in the late Ch'ing), Ling-nan hsueh-pao, 4.2: 57-102 (June 1935).

Ch'uan Han-sheng 全漢昇, "Ch'ing-mo fan-tui Hsi-hua ti yen-lun" 清末反對西化的言論 (Opinions expressed against Western culture at the end of the Ch'ing dynasty), Ling-nan hsueh-pao, 5.3-4: 122-166 (December 1936).

Ch'uan Han-sheng 全漢昇, "Ch'ing-mo Han-yang t'ieh-ch'ang" 清末漢陽鐵廠 (The Hanyang Iron and Steel Works, 1890-1908), She-hui k'o-hsueh lun-ts'ung 社會科學論叢 , no. 1: 1-33 (April 1950).

Ch'uan Han-sheng 全漢昇, "Ch'ing-chi ti Chiang-nan chih-tsao-chü" 清季的江南製造局 ("The Kiangnan Arsenal of the Ch'ing Dynasty"), Li-shih yü-yen yen-chiu-so chi-k'an 歷史語言研究所集刊 ("Bulletin of the Institute of History and Philology, Academia Sinica"), vol. 23, "Presented in memorial of Director Fu Ssu-nien", part 1 (Taipeh, 1951), pp. 145-159.

Ch'uan-kuo yin-hang nien-chien 全國銀行年鑑 (National banking yearbook), edited by Chung-kuo yin-hang (Bank of China), issue no. 3 (1936); no. 4 (1937).

Chuang Tzu, A new selected translation with an exposition of the philosophy of Kuo Hsiang, by Fung Yu-lan (Shanghai: Commercial Press, 1931), 164 pp.

Chuang Yǔ 莊俞 and Ho Sheng-nai 賀聖鼐 , ed., Tsui-chin san-shih-wu-nien chih Chung-kuo chiao-yü 最近三十五年之中國教育 (Chinese education in the last thirty-five years; Shanghai: Commercial Press, 1931), many hundred pages.

Ch'un-ch'iu Tso-chuan cheng-i 春秋左傳正義 (Established commentary on the Ch'un-ch'iu and Tso-chuan), 60 chüan, in Shih-san-ching chu-su 十三經注疏, ts'e 97-126 (1627-1639 edition), 160 ts'e.

Chung-kuo chien-she 中國建設 (China reconstruction), published in Shanghai, beginning 1930, monthly.

Chung-kuo chin-tai ching-chi-shih yen-chiu chi-k'an 中國近代經濟史研究集刊 (Studies in Modern Economic History of China; Peiping: Institute of Social Research, 1932-37), semi-annually.

Chung-kuo hsin-wen-hsueh ta-hsi, see Chao Chia-pi, A-ying.

Chung-kuo nien-chien 中國年鑑 (The China Year Book), comp. by Yuan Hsiang 阮湘 and others (first and only issue; Shanghai: Commercial Press, 1924), 2123 pp.

Chung-ying 仲英, ed., Yang-wu hsin-lun 洋務新論 (New essays on foreign affairs; 1894).

Chung-yung 中庸 (Doctrine of the Mean), annotated by Cheng Hsuan 鄭玄, 1 chüan, in Shih-san-ching chu 十三經注, ts'e 78, Chi-ku-lou edition (1852), 100 ts'e.

Clark, Grover, "The West goes to China and the remaking of her civilization begins", The Century Magazine, 114.2: 129-139 (June 1927).

(Constitution), see Tung-fang tsa-chih, special issue on constitutional government, January-February 1907. See also under Hsien-cheng.

Cordier, Henri, "La Mission Dubois de Jancigny dans l'Extrême-Orient," Revue de l'histoire des colonies françaises, 4: 130-133, 146, 148 (1916).

Costin, William Conrad, Great Britain and China 1833-1860 (Oxford: The Clarendon Press, 1937), 362 pp.

CSK : Ch'ing-shih kao 清史稿 (Draft history of the Ch'ing dynasty), compiled by Chao Erh-hsun and others, 536 chüan, in 131 ts'e. (Movable-type edition, 1927).

CSL : (Ch'ing shih-lu), Ta-Ch'ing li-ch'ao shih-lu 大清歷朝實錄 (Veritable records of the successive reigns of the Ch'ing dynasty), photolithographic edition, 1220 ts'e (Changchun, 1937).

CSLC : Ch'ing-shih lieh-chuan 清史列傳 (Historical biographies of the Ch'ing dynasty), compiled by Ch'ing-shih kuan, 80 ts'e (Shanghai: Chung-hua shu-chü movable-type edition, 1927).

CSPSR : Chinese Social and Political Science Review, published by The Chinese Social and Political Science Association, Peking, China, beginning April 1916, quarterly.

Danton, G. H., The Culture Contacts of the United States and China; the earliest Sino-American culture contacts, 1784-1844 (New York: Columbia University Press, 1931), 128 pp.

Davis, John Francis, China, during the war and since the peace, 2 vols. (London, 1852).

De Francis, John, Nationalism and Language Reform in China (Princeton: Princeton University Press, 1950), 306 pp.

Dunne, George H., "The Jesuits in China in the last days of the Ming Dynasty" (Ph. D. dissertation at the University of Chicago, 1944).

Evans, E. W. Price, Timothy Richard, a narrative of Christian enterprise and statesmanship in China (London: Carey Press, 1945), 160 pp.

Fairbank, J. K., Trade and Diplomacy on the China Coast: The Opening of the Treaty Ports, 1842-1854, 2 vols. (Cambridge, Mass.: Harvard University Press, 1953).

Fairbank, J.K., Ch'ing Documents, an introductory syllabus, 2 fascicles, multilith (Cambridge, Mass: Harvard University Press, 1952), 100 pp.

Fairbank, J. K., and Liu, K. C., Modern China: A Bibliographical Guide to Chinese Works 1898-1937, Harvard-Yenching Institute Studies, vol. I (Cambridge: Harvard University Press, 1950), 608 pp.

Fairbank, J. K., and Masataka Banno, Japanese Studies of Modern China, a bibliographical guide to research in history and social science (19th and 20th centuries), Harvard-Yenching Institute, to be published in 1954.

Fairbank, J. K., and Teng, S. Y., "On the Ch'ing tributary system," Harvard Journal of Asistic Studies, 6.2: 135-246 (June 1941).

Fan Wen-lan 范文瀾, Chung-kuo chin-tai shih 中國近代史 (A history of modern China; Peking: Hsin-hua shu-tien, 1949). Shang-pien or vol. A, 543 pp.

Fan Wen-lan 范文瀾, Han-chien kuei-tzu-shou Tseng Kuo-fan ti i-sheng 漢奸劊子手曾國藩的一生 (Life of the traitor and executioner Tseng Kuo-fan; Shanghai: Hsin-hua Book Company, 1949), 40 pp.

Fan Wen-lan, see also Wu Po.

Fang Hao 方豪, "Ch'ing-tai chin-i T'ien-chu-chiao so-shou Jih-pen chih ying-hsiang" 清代禁抑天主教所受日本之影响 (Japanese influence on the persecution of Catholicism during the Ch'ing Dynasty), in Fang Hao wen-lu, pp. 47-66.

Fang Hao 方豪, Chung-kuo T'ien-chu-chiao shih lun-ts'ung 中國天主教史論叢 (Essays on the history of Catholicism in China; Chungking: Commercial Press, 1944), 151 pp.

Fang Hao 方豪, Chung-wai wen-hua chiao-t'ung-shih lun-ts'ung 中外文化交通史論叢 (Essays on Sino-foreign cultural relations; Chungking: Tu-li ch'u-pan-she, 1944), 260 + 23 pp.

Fang Hao 方豪, Fang Hao wen-lu 方豪文錄 (Essays of Fang Hao; Shanghai: Shanghai Pien-i Kuan, 1948), 346 pp.

Fang Hao 方豪, "K'ang-hsi wu-shih-pa-nien Ch'ing-t'ing p'ai yuan ts'e-hui Liu-ch'iu ti-t'u chih yen-chiu" 康熙五十八年清廷派員測繪琉球地圖之研究 (On the cartographic survey of the Liu-ch'iu Islands by command of Emperor K'ang-hsi in 1719), Wen-shih-che hsueh-pao 文史哲學報 ("Bulletin of the College of Arts, National Taiwan University"), no. 1: 159-197 (June 1950).

Fang Hao 方豪, "Ming-mo Hsi-yang huo-ch'i liu-ju wo-kuo chih shih-liao" 明末西洋火器流入我國之史料 (Historical materials concerning the introduction of Western arms into China in the late Ming), Tung-fang tsa-chih, 40.1: 49-54 (January 1944).

Fang Hsien-t'ing 方顯廷 (H. D. Fong), Chung-kuo chih mien-fang-chih-yeh 中國之棉紡織業 (The Chinese cotton textile industry), published by the Kuo-li pien-i kuan (Shanghai: Commercial Press, 1934), 387 pp.

Fang Keng-sheng 方甦生, "Ch'ing lieh-ch'ao hou-fei chuan kao ting-pu" 清列朝后妃傳稿訂補 (Corrections and additions to Ch'ing lieh-ch'ao hou-fei chuan), Fu-jen hsueh-chih, 8.1: 99-112 (June 1939).

Feng Ch'eng-chün 馮承鈞, ed., Hai-lu chu 海錄注 (An annotated edition of the Hai-lu; Changsha: Commercial Press, 1938), 83 pp.

Feng Ching-t'ing hsing-chuang 馮景亭行狀 (A biography of Feng Kuei-fen), 1 ts'e, 19 leaves.

Feng Kuei-fen 馮桂芬, Chiao-pin-lu k'ang-i 校邠廬抗議 (Personal protests from the Study of Chiao-pin), 2 chüan (published in 1885, with an author's preface of 1861).

Feng Kuei-fen 馮桂芬, "Chih yang-ch'i i" 製洋器議 (On the manufacture of foreign weapons), in Chiao-pin-lu k'ang-i.

Feng Kuei-fen 馮桂芬, "Shan yü-i i" 善馭夷議 (On the better control of the barbarians), in Chiao-pin-lu k'ang-i.

Feng Kuei-fen 馮桂芬, "Ts'ai Hsi-hsueh i" 采西學議 (On the adoption of Western knowledge), in Chiao-pin-lu k'ang-i.

Feng Kuei-fen 馮桂芬, Hsien-chih-t'ang kao 顯志堂稿 (Literary works of Feng Kuei-fen), 12 chüan (published in 1877).

Feng Kuei-fen 馮桂芬, "Shang-hai she-li T'ung-wen Kuan i," 上海設立同文館議 (A proposal to establish a T'ung-wen Kuan in Shanghai), in Hsien-chih-t'ang kao.

Feng Kuei-fen, see also Feng Ching-t'ing, Huang Ts'ui-po.

Feng Yu-lan, see also Fung Yu-lan.

Feng Yu-lan (Derk Bodde, tr.), A Short History of Chinese Philosophy (Peiping: Henry Vetch, 1937), 454 pp.

Ferguson, John C., "The abolition of the competitive examinations in China," Journal of the American Oriental Society, 27: 79-87 (1906).

Fong, H. D., see Fang Hsien-t'ing.

Forke, Alfred von, Geschichte der neueren chinesischen Philosophie (Hamburg: Friederichsen, De Gruyter & Co., 1938), 693 pp.

Fortia d'Urban, Marquis de, La Chine et L'Angleterre (Paris, 1842).

Foster, John, "The Christian Origins of the Taiping Rebellion," The International Review of Missions 40: 156-167 (1951).

Franke, Wolfgang, "Die Staatspolitischen Reformversuche K'ang Yu-weis und seiner Schule. Ein Beitrag zur geistigen Auseinandersetzung Chinas mit dem Abendlande." Dissertation (Hamburg, 1935), 83 pp.

Franke, Wolfgang, "Juan Yuan (1764-1849)," Monumenta Serica 9: 53-80 (1944).

Fu-jen hsueh-chih 輔仁學誌 (Journal of Fu-jen University), published in Peiping, beginning 1929, semi-annual.

Fu Lan-ya 傅蘭雅 (John Fryer), Tso-chih ch'u-yen 佐治芻言 (Some advice on how to rule), in Hsi-cheng ts'ung-shu.

Fujiwara Sadamu 藤原定, Kindai Chūgoku shisō 近代中國思想 (Modern Chinese thought; Tōkyō: Shichōsha, 1948), 203 pp.

Fung Yu-lan, tr., Chuang Tzu, see Chuang Tzu, A new selected translation.

Giquel, Prosper, The Foochow Arsenal and its Results, from the Commencement in 1867 to the end of the Foreign Directorate on the 16th February, 1874, reprinted from the Shanghai Evening Courier, tr. by H. Lang (Shanghai, 1874), 38 pp.

Goodrich, L. Carrington, The Literary Inquisition of Ch'ien-Lung (Baltimore: Waverly Press, 1935), 275 pp.

Grosse-Aschhoff, Angelus, Negotiations between Ch'i-ying and Lagrené 1844-1846, Franciscan Institute Publications, Missiology Series, no. 2 (New York and Louvain, 1950), 195 pp.

Gundry, R. S., China Present and Past (London, 1895), 414 pp.

Haga Takeshi, 芳賀雄, Shina kōgyō shi 支那鑛業史 (History of Chinese mineral industry; Tōkyō: Dentsū shuppambu 電通出版部, 1943), 365 pp.

Hail, William James, Tseng Kuo-fan and the Taiping Rebellion (New Haven: Yale University Press, 1927), 422 pp.

Han Shao-su 韓少蘇, "T'an Tseng Chi-tse" 談曾紀澤 (A note on Tseng Chi-tse), Kuo-wen chou-pao, 12.25: 1-4 (July 1935).

Hart, Robert, These from the Land of Sinim, Essays on the Chinese Question (London, 1903), 302 pp.

Hart, Robert, see Ho-te.

Hattori Unokichi 服部宇之吉, Shinkoku tsūkō 清國通考 (A general account of the Ch'ing government), 2 vols. (Tōkyō: Sanseidō 三省堂, 1905), 166 & 204 pp.

Hibbert, Eloise Talcott, Jesuit Adventure in China: during the Reign of K'ang Hsi (New York: E. P. Dutton and Co., 1941), 291 pp.

Hirase Minokichi 平瀬巳之吉, Kindai Shina keizai shi 近代支那經濟史 (Modern Chinese economic history; Tōkyō: Chūō Kōronsha, 1942), 388 pp.

Hiratsuka Atsushi 平塚篤, comp., Zoku Itō Hirobumi hiroku 續伊藤博文祕錄 (Supplement to the collection of Itō's private documents; Tōkyō: Shunjūsha, 1930), 254 pp.

Hiyane Antei 比屋根安定, Shina Kirisuto-kyōshi 支那基篤教史 (History of Christianity in China; Tōkyō: Seikatsusha, 1940), 324 pp.

Ho Ch'ang-ling 賀長齡 comp., Huang-ch'ao ching-shih wen-pien 皇朝經世文編 (Essays of practical use to society during the Ch'ing dynasty), first printed in 1827, 120 chüan (Shanghai: Kuang-po-sung-chai edition, 1887).

Ho Ch'i 何啟 and Hu Li-yuan 胡禮垣, Hsin-cheng chen-ch'üan 新政真詮 (The true meaning of new government; Hongkong, 1895, reprinted, 1909).

Ho I-k'un 何貽焜, T'ing-lin hsueh-shuo shu-p'ing 亭林學說述評 (A presentation and comments on Ku Yen-wu's academic ideas; Chungking: Cheng-chung shu-chü, 1944), 305 pp.

Ho Ping-ti, "Weng T'ung-ho and the 'One Hundred Days of Reform,'" Far Eastern Quarterly, 10.2: 125-135 (February 1951).

Ho-te 赫德 (Hart, Robert) ed., Hsi-hsueh ju-men ts'ung-shu 西學入門叢書 (Collected works introductory to Western learning; 1886).

Ho-te 赫德 (Hart, Robert), P'ang-kuan san lun 旁觀三論 (Three essays by a spectator; Shanghai: Tung-pien ch'ai, 1898).

Hsi Wei and Chu Chi-yung ed., see Ku Yen-wu, T'ing-lin hsien-sheng i-shu hui-chi.

Hsi Yin 惜陰, "Keng-tzu ch'üan-huo tung-nan hu-pao chih chi-shih" 庚子拳禍東南互保之紀實 (A reliable account of the mutual protection [of foreigners and Chinese] in southeastern China during the Boxer Uprising), Jen-wen, 2.7: 1-7 (September 1931).

Hsi Yin 惜陰, "Shu Ho-fei i-wen" 書合肥軼聞 (Anecdotes about Li Hung-chang), Jen-wen, 3.7: 106 (1932).

44

Hsi Yü-fu 席裕福 ed., Huang-ch'ao cheng-tien lei-tsuan 皇朝政典類纂 (A classified compilation of political statutes of the Ch'ing dynasty), 500 chüan (Shanghai: T'u-shu chi-ch'eng chü, 1903).

Hsia K'ang-nung 夏康農 , Lun Hu Shih yü Chang Chün-mai 論胡適與張君勱 (On Hu Shih and Chang Chün-mai; Shanghai, 1948), 68 pp.

Hsia Yen-te, Chung-kuo chin-pai-nien ching-chi ssu-hsiang 夏炎德,中國近三百年經濟思想 (Chinese economic thought during the last hundred years; Shanghai: Commercial Press, 1948), 202 pp.

Hsiang Ta 向達 , Chung-Hsi chiao-t'ung shih 中西交通史 (A history of China's contact with the West; Shanghai: Chung-hua Book Co., 1934), 167 pp.

Hsiang Ta 向達 and others, T'ai-p'ing T'ien-kuo 太平天國 (Source materials about the Heavenly Kingdom of Great Peace), 8 vols., compiled by Hsiang Ta and more than ten others of the Chinese Historical Association and published by the Shen-chou kuo-kuang she 神州國光社 (Shanghai, 1952), 3389 pp.

Hsiao I-shan 蕭一山 , Ch'ing-tai t'ung-shih 清代通史 (A general history of the Ch'ing dynasty), 2 vols. (Shanghai: Commercial Press, 1927-28).

Hsiao I-shan 蕭一山 , Chin-tai mi-mi she-hui shih-liao 近代祕密社會史料 (Historical material on modern secret societies), 6 chüan (Peiping: The Peiping National Research Academy, 1935).

Hsiao I-shan 蕭一山 ed., T'ien-ch'ao t'ien-mu chih-tu 天朝田畝制度 (The land system of the Heavenly Dynasty), 1 chüan, in T'ai-ping T'ien-kuo ts'ung-shu, ts'e 4, (Shanghai: Commercial Press, 1936, 16 ts'e).

Hsiao I-shan 蕭一山 , Tseng Kuo-fan 曾國藩 (Chungking: Sheng-li ch'u-pan-she, 1944), 202 pp.

Hsiao I-shan 蕭一山 , Ch'ing-tai shih 清代史 (History of the Ch'ing Dynasty; Chungking: Commercial Press, 1945), 307 pp.

Hsiao I-shan 蕭一山 , "Huai-chün yü Hsiang-chün chih pieh" 淮軍與湘軍之別 (The difference between the Anhwei Army and the Hunan Army), Tzu-yueh ts'ung-k'an 子曰叢刊 , no. 1: 11-13 (1948).

Hsiao Kung-ch'üan 蕭公權 , Chung-kuo cheng-chih ssu-hsiang shih 中國政治思想史 (A history of Chinese political thought), 2 vols. (Shanghai: Commercial Press, 1946), 196 + 484 pp.

Hsiao San 蕭三 , Mao Tse-tung t'ung-chih ti ch'ing-shao-nien shih-tai 毛澤東同志的青少年時代 (The childhood and boyhood of comrade Mao Tse-tung; Peiping, 1949), 109 pp.

Hsieh Chao-chih 謝肇制 , Wu tsa-tsu 五雜俎 (Five desultory notes), in Wu-hang pao-shu t'ang 吳航寶樹堂 , undated block-print edition.

Hsieh En-hui 謝恩輝 , "Chang Hsiang-t'ao chih ching-chi chien-she" 張香濤之經濟建設 (Chang Hsiang-t'ao's economic reconstruction), Ching-chi hsueh-pao 經濟學報, no. 2: 105-148 (June 1941).

Hsieh Fu-ch'eng, see Hsueh Fu-ch'eng.

Hsieh Hsing-yao 謝興堯 ed., T'ai-p'ing T'ien-kuo ts'ung-shu 太平天國叢書 (Collection of works on the Taiping rebellion), 3 ts'e (Peiping: published by the editor, 1938).

Hsieh Kuo-chen 謝國楨 , Huang Li-chou hsueh-p'u 黃黎洲學譜 (A sketch of the scholarly work of Huang Tsung-hsi; Shanghai: Commercial Press, 1932), 176 pp.

Hsieh Kuo-chen 謝國楨 , Ku Ning-jen hsueh-p'u 顧寧人學譜 (A sketch of the scholarly work of Ku Yen-wu; 1930).

Hsieh Pin 謝彬, Chung-kuo yu-tien hang-k'ung shih 中國郵電航空史 (History of the post, telegraph and aviation in China; Shanghai: Chung-hua shu-chü, 1928), 262 pp.

Hsien-cheng tsa-shih 憲政雜識 (Constitutional government miscellany), 1.1 (December 1906).

Hsien Yung-hsi 冼榮熙, "Wu-shih-nien lai chih Han-yeh-p'ing" 五十年來之漢冶萍 (Han-yeh-p'ing Company during the past 50 years), Shih-tai kung-lun 時代公論, no. 52: 64-67 (March 1933).

Hsin-ch'ing-nien 新青年 (La Jeunesse), published in Peking, beginning 1915, monthly.

Hsing-shih chou-pao she 醒獅週報社, ed., Kuo-chia chu-i chiang-yen chi 國家主義講演集 (Collected lectures on Nationalism), 1 ts'e (Shanghai: Chung-hua Book Co., 1925).

Hsü Ch'ang-chih 徐昌治, Sheng-ch'ao p'o-hsieh chi 聖朝破邪集 (Collected works of the Sacred Dynasty exposing heterodoxy), 8 ts'e (Japanese block-print edition, 1855).

Hsü Chi-yü 徐繼畬, Ying-huan chih-lueh 瀛環志略 (A brief description of the oceans' circuit, completed in 1848 in 10 chüan (printed, 1850; reprinted, 1866).

Hsü Chi-yü 徐繼畬, Sung-k'an hsien-sheng ch'üan-chi 松龕先生全集 (Complete works of Hsü Chi-yü; 1915 edition).

Hsü Chih-liang 徐之良, "Chin-tai Chung-kuo wen-hua yun-tung ti kung-tsui" 近代中國文化運動的功罪 (Merits and demerits of the cultural movement in modern China), Chung-hua yueh-pao 中華月報, 7.5.

Hsü I-shih 徐一士, "T'an Li Ching-fang" 談李經方 (On Li Ching-fang), Kuo-wen chou-pao, 11.44:1-4 (November 1934).

Hsü I-shih 徐一士, "Tso Tsung-t'ang yü Liang Ch'i-ch'ao" 左宗棠與梁啟超 (Tso Tsung-t'ang and Liang Ch'i-ch'ao), Ku-chin, no. 14 (1942).

Hsü Jun 徐潤 (Hsü Yü-chih 雨之 or Chü Yü-chee), Hsü Yü-chai tzu-hsü nien-p'u, fu Shang-hai tsa-chi 徐愚齋自敘年譜，附上海雜記 (Autobiographical chronicle by Hsü Yü-chai, together with miscellaneous notes on Shanghai), published by the Hsü family (Hsiang-shan Hsü-shih 香山徐氏), postface by Kan To 闞鐸 dated 1927, pp. 135 + 31.

Hsü Keng-sheng 徐梗生, Chung-wai ho-pan mei-t'ieh-k'uang-yeh shih-hua 中外合辦煤鐵礦業史話 (Histories of Sino-foreign joint-managed coal and iron mines; Shanghai: Commercial Press, 1946), 270 pp.

Hsü Shou-ch'ang 許壽裳, Chang Ping-lin 章炳麟 (Chungking: Sheng-li ch'u-pan she, 1945), 172 pp.

Hsü, Shuhsi, China and Her Political Entity (New York: Oxford University Press, 1926), 438 pp.

Hsü Tsung-tse 徐宗澤, Ming-Ch'ing chien Yeh-su-hui-shih i-chu t'i-yao 明清間耶穌會士譯著提要 (An annotated bibliography of the works written or translated during the Ming and Ch'ing dynasties into Chinese by Jesuits; Shanghai: The Chung-hua Book Co., 1949), 482 pp.

Hsü T'ung-hsin, see Chang Chih-tung, Chang Wen-hsiang-kung nien-p'u.

Hsü Ying 徐盈, Tang-tai Chung-kuo shih-yeh jen-wu chih 當代中國實業人物志 (An account of contemporary Chinese industrialists; complete information unavailable, 1948).

Hsuan-t'ung cheng-chi 宣統政紀 (Records of the political administration of the Hsuan-t'ung period), 16 ts'e (Dairen: Liao-hai shu-she, preface written in 1934).

Hsueh Fu-ch'eng 薛福成, Yung-an ch'üan-chi 庸盦全集 (Collected works of Hsueh Fu-ch'eng), 21 chüan (Shanghai: Tsui-liu-t'ang 醉六堂 lithographic edition, 1897).

Hsueh Fu-ch'eng 薛福成, Ch'ou-yang ch'u-i 籌洋芻議 (Rough discussion of the management of foreign affairs), in Yung-an ch'üan-chi.

Hsueh Fu-cheng 薛福成, Ch'u-shih Ying Fa I Pi ssu-kuo jih-chi 出使英法意比四國日記 (Diary of a mission to the four countries of England, France, Italy and Belgium), 6 chüan (published, 1892; with a supplement, 1899; included in the collection Yung-an ch'üan-chi).

Hsueh Fu-ch'eng 薛福成, Yung-an pi-chi 庸盦筆記 (Desultory notes of Yung-an; first printed, 1895; also in Yung-an ch'üan-chi).

Hsueh Fu-ch'eng 薛福成, Ch'u-shih kung-tu 出使公牘 (Official correspondence from a mission abroad), 10 chüan (first published, 1897; reprinted in Yung-an ch'üan-chi).

Hsueh Fu-ch'eng 薛福成, Hai-wai wen-pien 海外文編 (Collection of essays of Hsueh Fu-ch'eng written overseas), 4 chüan, in Yung-an ch'üan-chi.

Hsueh Fu-ch'eng 薛福成, Yung-an wen-pien 庸盦文編 (Collected essays of Hsueh Fu-ch'eng), 4 chüan, in Yung-an ch'üan-chi.

Hsueh-lin 學林 (The academic world), published in Shanghai, beginning September 1921, monthly.

Hsueh-ssu 學思 (Learning and thinking), published in Chengtu, beginning 1942, semi-monthly.

Hu Chün 胡鈞, Chang Wen-hsiang-kung nien-p'u 張文襄公年譜 (A chronological biography of Chang Chih-tung), edited by Hu Chün 胡鈞 (Peking: T'ien-hua yin-shu-kuan, 1939), 6 chüan.

Hu Shih 胡適, Hu Shih wen-ts'un 胡適文存 (Collected essays of Hu Shih), 2 vols. (first collection, Shanghai, 1921).

Hu Shih 胡適, Hu Shih wen-ts'un erh-chi 胡適文存二集 (Second collection of the essays of Hu Shih), 2 vols. (Shanghai, 1924).

Hu Shih, "The Chinese Renaissance," China Year Book, 633-637 (1924).

Hu Shih 胡適, "Wo-men tui-yü Hsi-yang chin-tai wen-ming ti t'ai-tu" 我們對於西洋近代文明的態度 (Our attitude toward modern Western civilization), Tung-fang tsa-chih, 23.17: 73-82 (September 1926).

Hu Shih 胡適, Hu Shih wen-ts'un san-chi 胡適文存三集 (Third collection of the essays of Hu Shih), 4 vols. (Shanghai: Oriental Book Co., 1930).

Hu Shih 胡適, Ssu-shih tzu-shu 四十自述 (Autobiography at forty), vol. 1 (Shanghai: Ya-tung Book Co., 1933), 180 pp.

Hu Shih, The Chinese Renaissance (Chicago: University of Chicago Press, 1934), 110 pp.

Hu Shih 胡適, "Chi Ku Hung-ming" 記辜鴻銘 (On Ku Hung-ming), Ta-kung-pao, wen-i fu-k'an 文藝副刊, no. 164 (August 1935).

Hu Shih 胡適 ed., Chien-she li-lun chi 建設理論集 (Theoretical bases of [literary] reconstruction), vol. 1 of Chung-kuo hsin-wen-hsueh ta-hsi, see Chao Chia-pi.

Hu Shih 胡適, Ts'ang-hui-shih cha-chi 藏暉室劄記 (Notebook from the Hidden-brilliance Studio), 4 vols. (Shanghai: Ya-tung Book Co., 1939; new edition, Shanghai: the Commercial Press, 1948).

Hu Shih 胡適, Hu Shih liu-hsueh jih-chi 胡適留學日記 (Hu Shih's diary when he studied abroad), 4 ts'e (Shanghai: Commercial Press, second printing, 1948).

Hu Yuan-chün 胡遠濬, "T'an Ssu-t'ung Jen-hsueh chih p'i-p'ing" 譚嗣同仁學之批評 (A comment on T'an Ssu-t'ung's Jen-hsueh), Kuo-li chung-yang ta-hsueh pan-yueh-k'an 國立中央大學半月刊, 2.1: 109-119 (October 1930).

Hua Kang 華岡, Wu-ssu yun-tung shih 五四運動史 (A history of the May Fourth Movement; Shanghai: Hai-yen shu-tien, 1951), 220 pp.

Hua Ying-shen 華應申, Chung-kuo Kung-ch'an-tang lieh-shih chuan 中國共產黨烈士傳 (Biographies of Chinese Communist Party martyrs; Hongkong: Hsin-min-chu shu-chü, 1949), 224 pp.

Huang-Ch'ing chih-kung t'u 皇清職貢圖 (Illustrations of the regular tributaries of the imperial Ch'ing dynasty ; palace edition, 1761).

(Huang Jen-chi 黃仁濟), Huang-shih li-shih chi 黃氏歷事記 (An historical account of Huang Jen-chi; publisher and date unavailable).

Huang Ju-ch'eng 黃汝成, comp., Jih-chih lu chi-shih 日知錄集釋 (Collected commentaries on Jih-chih lu), 32 chüan (Shanghai: Chung-hua shu-chü, 1927).

Huang Li-chou, see Huang Tsung-hsi.

Huang Ti 黃迪, "Wu-ssu i-lai chih Chung-kuo hsueh-ch'ao" 五四以來之中國學潮 (Chinese student strikes since the May Fourth Movement), She-hui hsueh-chieh, vol. 6: 287-303 (June 1932).

Huang Ts'ui-po 黃淬伯, "Ch'i-shih-nien ch'ien chih wei-hsin jen-wu Feng Ching-t'ing" 七十年前之維新人物馮景亭 (Feng Kuei-fen, the reformer of seventy years ago), in Chung-shan wen-hua chiao-yü kuan chi-k'an 中山文化教育館季刊, 4.3:969-991 (1937).

Huang Tsun-hsien 黃遵憲, Jen-ching-lu shih-ts'ao 人境廬詩草 (Poems of Huang Tsun-hsien), 11 chüan (Peiping, 1930).

Huang Tsun-hsien 黃遵憲, Jih-pen-kuo chih 日本國志. (History of Japan), 10 ts'e (1890).

Huang Tsun-hsien, see Wen T'ing-ching.

Huang Tsung-hsi 黃宗羲, Ming-i tai-fang lu 明夷待訪錄, written in 1663, Ssu-pu pei-yao edition.

Huang Tsung-hsi 黃宗羲, Li-chou i-chu hui-k'an 梨洲遺著彙刊 (Collected writings of Huang Tsung-hsi), compiled by Hsueh Feng-ch'ang 薛鳳昌, including 29 titles, 20 ts'e (Shanghai: Shih-chung shu-chü movable type edition, 1910).

Huang Yen-yü, "Viceroy Yeh Ming-ch'en and the Canton Episode (1856-1861)," Harvard Journal of Asiatic Studies, 6.1: 37-127 (March 1941).

Hubbard, G. E., Eastern Industrialization and its Effect on the West (London: Oxford University Press, 1935), 395 pp.;(revised ed., 1938), 418 pp.

Hughes, E.R., The Invasion of China by the Western World (London: Adam and Charles Black, 1937), 324 pp.

Hummel, Arthur W., ed., Eminent Chinese of the Ch'ing Period (1644-1912), 2 vols. (Washington: The Library of Congress, 1943-1944).

Hummel, Arthur W., Jr., "Yuan Shih-k'ai as an Official under the Manchus," M.A. thesis (University of Chicago, 1949), 179 pp.

Hummel, William F., "K'ang Yu-wei, historical critic and social philosopher, 1857-1927," Pacific Historical Review, 4.4: 343-355 (December 1935).

Hung Jen-kan 洪仁玕, Tzu-cheng hsin-p'ien 資政新篇 (A new work for aid in administration; 1859). A photolithographic reproduction in I-ching 逸經, nos. 17-19 (1936); also in T'ai-p'ing T'ien-kuo, compiled by Hsiang Ta et al., Vol. II, pp. 521-541.

Hung Shen 洪琛, "Shen-pao tsung-tsuan ch'ang-mao chuang-yuan Wang T'ao" 申報總纂長毛狀元王韜 (Collection of material from Shen-pao on Wang T'ao, leading scholar among the long-haired rebels [Taipings]), Wen-hsueh 文學, 2.3 (1934) and 2.6.

Hussey, Harry, Venerable Ancestor; the life and times of Tz'u-hsi, 1835-1908, Empress of China (Garden City, N. Y.: Doubleday, 1949), 354 pp.

Ichiko Chūzō 市古宙三, "Giwaken no seikaku" 義和拳の性格 (The character of the Boxer movement), Kindai Chūgoku kenkyū (Research on Modern China), ed. by Niida Noboru 仁井田陞 and others (Tōkyō: Kōgakusha, 1948, 361 pp.), 245-267.

I-ching 逸經, published in Shanghai, beginning 1936, semi-monthly.

Ikeda Tōsen 池田桃川, "Itō kō to Ri Kō-shō" 伊藤公卜李鴻章 (Prince Itō and Li Hung-chang), Tōyō 東洋, 35.9: 124-131 (1932).

Inada Masatsugu 稻田正次, "Bojutsu seihen ni tsuite" 戊戌政變について (On the reform movement of 1898), Kindai Chūgoku Kenkyū (Research on Modern China), ed. by Niida Noboru 仁井田陞 and others (Tōkyō: Kōgahuska, 1948, 361 pp.), pp. 207-242.

Ishida Mikinosuke 石田幹之助, "Shina bunka to Seihō bunka to no kōryū" 支那文化と西方文化との交流 (The confluence of Chinese and Western culture), Iwanami kōza tōyō shichō 岩波講座東洋史潮 (Tōkyō: Iwanami, 1936), 153 pp.

I-shih 一士, "Jung-lu yü Yuan Shih-k'ai" 榮祿與袁世凱 (Jung-lu and Yuan Shih-k'ai), I-ching, no. 22: 25-28 (1937).

Ishihara Michihiro 石原道博, Mimmatsu Shinsho Nihon kisshi no kenkyū 明末清初日本乞師の研究 (A study of China's solicitation of military help from Japan in the late Ming and early Ch'ing; Tōkyō: Fuzambō 冨山房, 1945), 542 pp.

Itano Chōhachi 板野長八, "Kō Yū-i no daidō shisō" 康有爲の大同思想 (The Ta-t'ung idea of K'ang Yu-wei), Kindai Chūgoku Kenkyū (Tōkyō: Kōgakusha, 1948, 361 pp.), pp. 165-204.

Itano Chōhachi 板野長八, "Ryō Kei-chō no daidō shisō" 梁啟超の大同思想 ("The Idea of Ta-t'ung of Liang Ch'i-ch'ao"), pp. 69-84 in Wada hakushi kanreki kinen Tōyōshi ronsō 和田博士還曆記念東洋史論叢 (Collected essays in East Asian history, a memorial for the sixtieth birthday of Dr. Wada Sei; Tōkyō: Dainippon Yūbenkai Kōdansha, 1951), 806 + 71 pp.

IWSM : Ch'ou-pan i-wu shih-mo 籌辦夷務始末 (A complete account of the management of barbarian affairs), 260 chüan (Peking: printed by the Palace Museum in 1929-1931).

Izushi Yoshihiko 出石誠彥, Tōyō kinseishi kenkyū 東洋近世史研究 (Researches in the modern history of East Asia; Tōkyō: Taikandō 大觀堂, 1944), 387 pp.

Jansen, Marius B., "The Japanese and the Chinese Revolutionary Movement 1895-1915" (Harvard doctoral thesis in History, 1950), 320 pp. To be published, revised, under the title Adventurers and Revolutionaries: The Japanese and Sun Yat-sen, by the Harvard University Press in 1954.

Jen-chien-shih 人間世, published in Shanghai, beginning 1934, semi-monthly.

Jen-wen 人文 (Humanities), published in Shanghai, beginning 1930, monthly.

Juan Yuan 阮元, Tseng-tzu shih-p'ien chu-shih 曾子十篇注釋 (A commentary on the ten chapters of Tseng-tzu), 1 chüan, Hsiao-i chia-shu ts'ung-shu 孝義家塾叢書.

Juan Yuan 阮元, Ch'ou-jen chuan 疇人傳 (Biographies of scientists [especially astronomers and mathematicians]), 46 chüan (Wen-hsuan-lou ts'ung-shu 文選樓叢書 edition, 1799).

Jung Chao-tsu 容肇祖, "Lü Liu-liang chi ch'i ssu-hsiang" 呂留良及其思想 (Lü Liu-liang and his ideas), Fu-jen hsueh-chih, 5. 1-2: 1-85 (December 1936).

Kan Tso-lin 甘作霖, "Chiang-nan chih-tsao-chü chien-shih" 江南製造局簡史 (A brief history of the Kiangnan Arsenal), Tung-fang tsa-chih, 11.5: 46-48 (November 1914), and 11.6: 21-25 (December 1914).

K'ang-hsi yü Lo-ma shih-chieh kuan-hsi wen-shu 康熙與羅馬使節關係文書 (Documents relating to K'ang-hsi and the Tournon Legation from Rome), in Wen-hsien ts'ung-pien no. 6.

K'ang Yu-wei 康有爲, K'ang Nan-hai wen-chi hui-pien 康南海文集彙編 (Collected works of K'ang Yu-wei), 8 ts'e (Shih-huan shu-chü, 1925).

K'ang Yu-wei 康有爲, K'ang Nan-hai wen-ch'ao 康南海文鈔 (The writings of K'ang Yu-wei), in Tang-tai pa-ta-chia wen-ch'ao 當代八大家文鈔, ts'e 3-6, (1926).

K'ang Yu-wei 康有爲, Kung-ch'e shang-shu chi 公車上書記 (The memorial presented by the examination candidates), 1 ts'e (Shanghai, 1895).

K'ang Yu-wei 康有爲, K'ung-tzu kai-chih k'ao 孔子改制考 (Confucius as a reformer), 21 chüan, in 6 ts'e (Peking, 1923 edition).

K'ang Yu-wei 康有爲, Ta-t'ung shu 大同書 (A book on the universal commonwealth), compiled by Ch'ien Ting-an 錢定安 (Chung-hua Book Co., 1932).

K'ang Yu-wei, see Wu Tse.

Kao Liang-tso 高良佐, "Ch'ing-tai min-tsu ssu-hsiang chih hsien-tao-che" 清代民族思想之先導者 (Leading thinkers on nationalism during the Ch'ing period), Chien-kuo yueh-k'an, 9.5: 1-10 (November 1933).

Kao Nai-t'ung 高乃同, Ts'ai Chieh-min hsien-sheng chuan-lueh 蔡孑民先生傳略 (A brief biography of Mr. Ts'ai Yuan-p'ei; Chungking: Commercial Press, 1932).

Kayano Chōchi 萱野長知, Chūka minkoku kakumei hikyu 中華民國革命秘笈 (Confidential material concerning the revolution of the Republic of China), complete information unavailable.

Kent, P. H., Railway Enterprise in China; an account of its origin and development (London, 1907), 304 pp.

Kiang, Wen-han (Chiang Wen-han), The Chinese Student Movement (New York: King's Crown Press, 1948), 176 pp.

Ko Hsien-ning 葛賢寧, "Chin-tai Chung-kuo min-tsu shih-jen Huang Kung-tu" 近代中國民族詩人黃公度 (The nationalist poet Huang Kung-tu [Huang Tsun-hsien] of modern China), Hsin Chung-hua, 2.7: 91-101 (1934).

Ko Kung-chen 戈公振, Chung-kuo pao-hsueh shih 中國報學史 (History of Chinese Journalism; Shanghai: Commercial Press, 1927), 385 pp.

Kondō Haruo 近藤春雄, Gendai Chūgoku no sakka to sakuhin 現代中國の作家と作品 (Contemporary Chinese writers and writings; Tōkyō: Shinsen 1949), 380 pp.

Ko Shih-chün 葛世濬, Huang-ch'ao ching-shih-wen hsü-pien 皇朝經世文續編 (Supplement to the Huang-ch'ao ching-shih-wen), 120 chüan in 32 ts'e (Shanghai: T'u-shu chi-ch'eng chü movable type edition, 1888).

Ku-chin 古今 (Ancient and modern), published in Shanghai, beginning 1942, semi-monthly.

Ku-chin t'u-shu chi-ch'eng 古今圖書集成 (Compilation of books and illustrations of ancient and modern times), 10,000 chüan, plus a table of contents in 40 chüan (Completed, 1726; printed, 1728).

Ku Ch'un-fan 谷春帆, Chiu wen-ming yü hsin kung-yeh 舊文明與新工業 (Old civilization and new industry; Shanghai: Commercial Press, 1944), 213 pp.

Ku Hung-ming, Papers From a Viceroy's Yamen (Shanghai: Shanghai Mercury, 1901), 197 pp.

Ku Hung-ming 辜鴻銘, Tu I ts'ao-t'ang wen-chi 讀易草堂文集 (Collected essays of Ku Hung-ming), 1 ts'e (block print edition, 1922).

Ku Hung-ming, see Wen Yuan-ning, Yuan Chen-ying.

Ku Yen-wu 顧炎武, T'ien-hsia chün-kuo li-ping shu 天下郡國利病書 (A book on the [strategic and economic] advantages and disadvantages of the counties and states of the Empire), 120 chüan in 24 ts'e (Ssu-pu ts'ung-k'an edition, third series; author's preface dated 1662).

Ku Yen-wu 顧炎武, Jih-chih lu 日知錄 (Notes of daily [accumulation] of knowledge), first printed by him in 8 chüan in 1670. After revisions, it was printed in Fukien in 1695 in the present form of 32 chüan, and re-published in 1872 by Ch'ung-wen shu-chü in Hupei, 16 ts'e.

Ku Yen-wu 顧炎武, T'ing-lin hsien-sheng i-shu hui-chi 亭林先生遺書彙輯 (Collected writings of Ku Yen-wu), compiled by Hsi Wei 席威 and Chu Chi-yung 朱記榮, 24 ts'e (block-print edition of Chu's Chiao-ching shan-fang 朱氏校經山房, 1888).

Ku Yen-wu 顧炎武, "Chün-hsien lun" 郡縣論, in T'ing-lin shih-wen ch'üan-chi 亭林詩文全集 (Collected works of Ku Yen-wu), 4 ts'e (Ssu-pu pei-yao edition, 1930).

Kung Chün 龔駿, Chung-kuo hsin-kung-yeh fa-chan-shih ta-kang 中國新工業發展史大綱 (Outline history of the development of modern industry in China; Shanghai: Commercial Press, 1933), 302 pp.

"Kung-ssu" 公司 (Corporations), see Chung-kuo nien-chien 中國年鑑 (The China Year Book), pp. 1587-1614.

Kuo Chan-po 郭湛波, Chin wu-shih-nien Chung-kuo ssu-hsiang shih 近五十年中國思想史 (A history of Chinese thought during the last fifty years; Peiping: Jen-wen shu-tien, 1936), 432 pp.

Kuo-feng 國風 (The National Spirit), published in Chungking, beginning 1942, semi-monthly.

Kuo-li chung-yang yen-chiu yuan 國立中央研究院 (Academia Sinica), Ch'ing-chu Ts'ai Yuan-p'ei hsien-sheng liu-shih-wu sui lun-wen chi 慶祝蔡元培先生六十五歲論文集 (Studies presented to Ts'ai Yuan-p'ei on his sixty-fifth birthday), Li-shih yü-yen yen-chiu-so chi-k'an wai-pien ti-i chung 歷史語言研究所集刊外編第一種 (Supplement no. 1 of the Journal of the Institute of History and Philology), 2 vols. (Peiping, 1938).

Kuo, P. C., A Critical Study of the First Anglo-Chinese War with Documents (Shanghai: The Commercial Press, 1930), 315 pp.

Kuo Pin-chia 郭斌佳, "Keng-tzu ch'üan-luan" 庚子拳亂 (The Boxer Rebellion of 1900), Kuo-li Wu-han ta-hsueh wen-che chi-k'an 國立武漢大學文哲季刊 ("Quarterly Journal of Liberal Arts") 6.1: 135-182 (1936).

Kuo Pin-ho 郭斌龢, "Yen Chi-tao" 嚴幾道 (Yen Fu), Kuo-feng, 8.6: 213-228 (1936).

Kuo Sung-tao 郭嵩燾, Kuo shih-lang tsou-shu 郭侍郎奏疏 (The memorials of Kuo Sung-tao), 12 chüan (1892 edition).

Kuo Sung-tao 郭嵩燾, Yang-chih shu-wu ch'üan-chi 養知書屋全集 (Collected works of Kuo Sung-tao), 55 chüan (printed 1892).

Kuo Sung-tao 郭嵩燾, Yü-ch'ih lao-jen tzu-hsü 玉池老人自叙 (Autobiographical notes of Kuo Sung-tao), 1 chüan (1893 edition).

Kuo T'ing-i 郭廷以, Chin-tai Chung-kuo shih 近代中國史 (Modern Chinese history; Shanghai: Commercial Press, 1940), 635 pp.

Kuo T'ing-i 郭廷以, T'ai-p'ing T'ien-kuo shih-shih jih-chih 太平天國史事日誌 (History of the Taiping Kingdom, a daily record), 2 vols. (Chungking and Shanghai: Commercial Press, 1946).

Kuo-wen chou-pao 國聞週報 (National news weekly), published in Tientsin, beginning 1924, weekly.

La Fargue, Thomas E., "Chinese Educational Commission to the United States, A Government Experiment in Western Education," Far Eastern Quarterly, 1.1: 59-70 (November 1941).

La Fargue, Thomas E., China's First Hundred (Pullman: State College of Washington, 1942), 176 pp.

Langer, W. L., The Diplomacy of Imperialism, 1890-1902, 2 vols. (New York and London: A. A. Knopf, 1935); second edition (1951), 797 pp.

Lao Kan 勞幹, "Ts'ai Yuan-p'ei yü Pei-ching ta-hsueh" 蔡元培與北京大學 (Ts'ai Yuan-p'ei and Peking University), Kuo-wen chou-pao, 3.36: 1-5 (1926).

Lao Nai-hsuan 勞乃宣, Ch'üan-an san-chung 拳案三種 (Three works on the Boxer Case; block-print edition of 1902).

Lao Nai-hsuan 勞乃宣, I-ho-ch'üan chiao-men yuan-liu k'ao 義和拳教門源流考 (A study of the origin of the I-ho-ch'üan), reprinted in Tso Shun-sheng, Chung-kuo chin-pai-nien shih tzu-liao hsü-pien, vol. 1.

Latourette, K. S., A History of Christian Missions in China (London: Society for promoting Christian knowledge, 1929), 930 pp.

Lee, Shiu-keung, Timothy Richard and the Reform Movement in China (Hartford Theological Seminary), complete information unavailable.

Legge, James, The Chinese Classics, 8 vols. (Oxford: Clarendon Press, 1893-1895).

Levenson, Joseph R., "The breakdown of Confucianism: Liang Ch'i-ch'ao before exile—1873-1898," Journal of the History of Ideas, 11.4: 448-485 (October 1950).

Levenson, Joseph R., Liang Ch'i-ch'ao and the Mind of Modern China (Cambridge: Harvard University Press, 1953).

Levy, M. J., and Shih Kuo-heng, The Rise of the Modern Chinese Business Class (New York: International Secretariat, Institute of Pacific Relations, 1949), 63 pp.

Li, Ch'iao-p'ing, The Chemical Arts of Old China (Easton, Pa.: Journal of Chemical Education, 1948), 215 pp.

Li Chien-nung 李劍農, Chung-kuo chin-pai-nien cheng-chih shih 中國近百年政治史 (The political history of China during the last hundred years), 2 vols. (Shanghai: Commercial Press, 1947).

Li Hung-chang 李鴻章, Li Wen-chung-kung ch'üan-chi 李文忠公全集 (A complete collection of the works of Li Hung-chang), 100 ts'e (Shanghai, 1921).

Li Hung-chang 李鴻章, Li Wen-chung-kung tsou-kao 李文忠公奏稿, in Li Wen-chung-kung ch'üan-chi, ts'e 2-51.

Li Hung-chang 李鴻章 , Li Wen-chung-kung p'eng-liao han-kao 李文忠公朋僚函稿 , in Li Wen-chung-kung ch'üan-chi, ts'e 52-61.

Li Hung-chang 李鴻章 , "Ch'ou-i chih-tsao lun-ch'uan wei-k'o ts'ai-ch'e che" 籌議製造輪船未可裁撤摺 (Planning the construction of steamships should not be given up), in Li Wen-chung-kung tsou-kao.

(Li Hung-chang 李鴻章), "Li Wen-chung-kung Hung-chang nien-p'u" 李文忠公鴻章年譜 (A chronological biography of Li Hung-chang), comp. by Li Shu-ch'un 李書春 , Shih-hsueh nien-pao 史學年報 , no. 1: 97-124 (July 1929).

Li Hung-chang, see Wu Pao-chang.

Li Ki (The Book of Rites), tr. by James Legge, ed. by F. Max Muller, in The Sacred Books of China: The Texts of Confucianism, 2 vols. (Oxford, 1885).

Li-ma-tou 俐瑪竇 (Matteo Ricci), T'ien-chu shih-i 天主實義 (The true meaning of Christianity), 2 chüan (Sheng-shih-t'ang movable type edition, 1922).

Li Ming 李明 and others, Chung-kung liu-lieh-shih hsiao-chuan 中共六烈士小傳 (Brief biographies of six Chinese communist martyrs; Hongkong: The New China Bookstore, 1949), 84 pp.

Li P'ei-en 李培恩 , "Chin-pai-nien lai Chung-kuo chih yin-hang" 近百年來中國之銀行 (Chinese banking in the past hundred years), Hsueh-lin, no. 9: 1-14 (July 1941).

Li Shih-ch'en 李石岑 , Jen-sheng che-hsueh 人生哲學 (Philosophy of life; Shanghai: Commercial Press, 1926).

Li Shou-ch'ang 李守常 , P'ing-min chu-i 平民主義 ("Democracy"; Shanghai, 1925), 35 pp.

Li Shu-ch'ang, comp., see (Tseng Kuo-fan), Tseng Wen-cheng-kung nien-p'u.

Li Shu-ch'un, comp., see Li Hung-chang, "Li Wen-chung-kung Hung-chang nien-p'u."

Li Ta-chao 李大釗 . "Bolshevism ti sheng-li" Bolshevism 的勝利 , Hsin-ch'ing-nien, 5.5: 442-448 (November 15, 1918).

Li Ta-chao 李大釗 , "Wo-ti Ma-k'o-ssu chu-i kuan" 我的馬克思主義觀 (My view of Marxism), Hsin-ch'ing-nien, 6.5: 521-537 (May, 1919).

Li Ta-chao, see Yang Yung-kuo.

Li T'i-mo-t'ai 李提摩太 (Timothy Richard), Hsi-to 西鐸 (The warning bell from the West), 1 chüan. (Shanghai: Kwang-hsueh hui, printed 1895). For a further list of his Chinese writings, see catalogue of the Chinese-Japanese Library, Harvard University.

Li Ting-fang 李鼎芳 , Tseng Kuo-fan chi ch'i mu-fu jen-wu 曾國藩及其幕府人物 (Tseng Kuo-fan and his secretarial personnel; Kweiyang: Wen-t'ung shu-chü, 1946).

Li Wen-chung-kung, see Li Hung-chang.

Li Yeh 李冶 , "Ts'e yuan-hai ching" 測圓海鏡 , ch. 107 of Ssu-k'u ch'üan-shu tsung-mu t'i-yao 四庫全書總目提要 (Tai-tung shu-chü edition).

Li Yen 李儼 , Chung-kuo shu-hsueh ta-kang 中國數學大綱 (Outline of Chinese mathematics), vol. 1 (Shanghai, 1931), 222 pp.

Li Yen 李儼, Chung-kuo suan-hsueh shih 中國算學史 (History of mathematics in China; Shanghai: Commercial Press, 1937), 293 pp.

Li Yen 李儼, Chung-suan-shih lun-ts'ung 中算史論叢 (Essays on the history of mathematics in China), in 4 series, 1931-1947 (first series, 1931, 408 pp.; 2nd series, 1935, 474 pp.; 3rd. series, 1935, 400 pp.; 4th. series, 2 vols., 1947, 638 pp.).

Li Yuan-tu 李元度, Kuo-ch'ao hsien-cheng shih-lueh 國朝先正事略 (Biographies of leading statesmen and men of letters of the Ch'ing period), 60 chüan (published, 1866).

(Liang Ch'i-ch'ao 梁啟超), "Hsin-min shuo i" 新民説 (The renovation of the people), Hsin-min ts'ung-pao 新民叢報, no. 1: 1-10 (January 1902).

Liang Ch'i-ch'ao 梁啟超, Hsi-hsueh shu-mu piao 西學書目表 (A bibliography of books on Western knowledge), in Chih-hsueh ts'ung-shu ch'u-chi 質學叢書初集, ts'e 9-10.

Liang Ch'i-ch'ao 梁啟超, K'ang Nan-hai chuan 康南海傳 (Biography of K'ang Yu-wei), 1 ts'e (Shanghai, 1908).

Liang Ch'i-ch'ao 梁啟超, Yin-ping-shih ho-chi 飲冰室合集 (Collected works of the Ice-drinkers' Studio [Liang Ch'i-ch'ao]), includes Wen-chi 文集 (Collection of essays), ts'e 1-16, Chuan-chi 專集 (Special collection), ts'e 17-40 (also numbered ts'e 1-24); 40 ts'e (Shanghai: Chunghua shu-chü, 1936).

Liang Ch'i-ch'ao 梁啟超, Ssu-shih-nien lai ta-shih chi 四十年來大事記 (Important events in the last forty years [biography of Li Hung-chang]), ts'e 18 of Yin-ping-shih ho-chi.

Liang Ch'i-ch'ao 梁啟超, Ou-yu hsin-ying lu chieh-lu 歐遊心影錄節錄 (A record of impressions during travel in Europe) in Yin-ping-shih ho-chi, ts'e 21.

Liang Ch'i-ch'ao 梁啟超, Ch'ing-tai hsueh-shu kai-lun 清代學術概論 (A general discussion of the academic learning of the Ch'ing dynasty), in Yin-ping-shih ho-chi, ts'e 25.

Liang Ch'i-ch'ao 梁啟超, Chung-kuo chin-san-pai-nien hsueh-shu shih 中國近三百年學術史 (A history of Chinese academic thought during the last three hundred years; Shanghai, 1926), 562 pp. Also in Yin-ping-shih ho-chi, ts'e 33. A resumé in English was published as "An Outline of the Chinese Cultural History of the Last Three Centuries," CSPSR 7.3: 33-47 (July, 1924).

Liang Ch'i-ch'ao 梁啟超, Chu Shun-shui hsien-sheng nien-p'u 朱舜水先生年譜 (A chronological biography of Chu Shun-shui), in Yin-ping-shih ho-chi, ts'e 38, or Chuan-chi, ts'e 22.

Liang Ch'i-ch'ao 梁啟超, "Wu-shih-nien Chung-kuo chin-hua kai-lun" 五十年中國進化概論 (A brief discussion of progress in China during the past fifty years), in Yin-ping-shih ho-chi, Wen-chi, part 39.

Liang Ch'i-ch'ao 梁啟超, "Lao-tzu che-hsueh" 老子哲學 (The philosophy of Lao-tzu), in Yin-ping-shih ho-chi, Wen-chi, part 63.

Liang Ch'i-ch'ao 梁啟超, "Tung-nan ta-hsueh k'o-pi kao-pieh tz'u" 東南大學課畢告別辭 (Parting speech after completing classes at Tung-nan University), in Yin-ping-shih ho-chi, Wen-chi, part 70.

Liang Ch'i-ch'ao, see Wu Ch'i-ch'ang; Wu Tse; Itano.

(Liang Shih-i 梁士詒), San-shui Liang Yen-sun hsien-sheng nien-p'u 三水梁燕孫先生年譜 (A chronological biography of Liang Shih-i of San-shui), ed. by Liang's disciples (published [by Liang's family members] 1939; 2nd printing, 1946), 624 pp.

Library of Congress, Bibliography of Modern Chinese Law in the Library of Congress (1944), 49 mimeographed pages.

Lin Mou-sheng, Men and Ideas, an informal history of Chinese political thought (New York: John Day Co., 1942), 256 pp.

Lin, T. C., "Li Hung-chang, his Korea Policies 1870-1885", CSPSR, 19.2: 200-233 (1935).

Lin Tse-hsü 林則徐, Lin Wen-chung-kung cheng-shu 林文忠公政書 (Collection of memorials by Lin Tse-hsü), 37 chüan (printed by the author's family).

Lin Tse-hsü 林則徐, "Lin Tse-hsü fu Wu Tzu-hsü pien-hsiu shu" 林則徐復吳子序編修書 (A reply from Lin Tse-hsü to the Hanlin Compiler Wu Tzu-hsü), in Li-tai ming-jen shu-cha hsü-pien 歷代名人書札續編, compiled by Wu Tseng-ch'i 吳曾祺 (Shanghai, 1909; 17th printing, 1925), 2 A. 18-19.

Lin Tse-hsü 林則徐, Lin Wen-chung-kung nien-p'u 林文忠公年譜 (A chronological biography of Lin Tse-hsü), comp. by Wei Ying-ch'i 魏應麒 (Shanghai: Commercial Press, 1935), 200 pp.

Lin Wen-chung-kung, see Lin Tse-hsü.

Lin Yao-hua 林耀華, "Yen Fu she-hui ssu-hsiang" 嚴復社會思想 (Social thought of Yen Fu), She-hui hsueh-chieh, 7: 1-82 (1933).

Lin Yü-t'ang 林語堂, "Ku Hung-ming" 辜鴻銘 (Ku Hung-ming), Jen-chien shih, no. 12: 37-40 (September 1934).

Lin Yutang, A History of the Press and Public Opinion in China (Chicago: University of Chicago Press, 1936).

Linebarger, Paul M. A., The Political Doctrines of Sun Yat-sen (Baltimore: Johns Hopkins Press, 1937), 273 pp.

Ling-nan hsueh-pao 嶺南學報 (Lingnan Journal), published by Lingnan University, Canton, beginning 1929, quarterly.

Liu Chin-tsao 劉錦藻, Ch'ing-ch'ao hsü wen-hsien t'ung-k'ao 清朝續文獻通考 (A supplement to the Wen-hsien t'ung-k'ao of the Ch'ing), the Commercial Press edition of the Shih-t'ung 十通

Liu Hsi-hung 劉錫鴻, Ying-yao jih-chi 英軺日記 (Diary of a mission to England), in Ling-chien-ko ts'ung-shu 靈鶼閣叢書, published by Chiang Piao 江標, ts'e 10; also in Hsiao-fang-hu-chai yü-ti ts'ung-ch'ao, ts'e 56.

Liu Hsi-san 劉錫三, "Wu-ssu i-hou Chung-kuo ko-p'ai ssu-hsiang-chia tui-yü Hsi-yang wen-ming ti t'ai-tu" 五四以後中國各派思想家對於西洋文明的態度 (Attitude of Chinese thinkers of various groups toward Western civilization after the May Fourth movement), She-hui hsueh-chieh, 7: 271-317 (June 1933).

Liu Hsiung-hsiang 劉熊祥, Ch'ing-chi shih-nien chih lien-E cheng-ts'e 清季十年之聯俄政策 (Russian alliance policy during the last decade of the Ch'ing Dynasty; Chungking: San-yu shu-tien, 1943).

Liu Hsiung-hsiang 劉熊祥, Ch'ing-chi ssu-shih-nien wai-chiao yü hai-fang 清季四十年外交與海防 (Forty years of foreign relations and coastal defense in the late Ch'ing period; alternative title, "A Study of the Tsungli Yamen"; Chungking: San-yu shu-tien, 1944), 182 pp.

(Liu Ming-ch'uan 劉銘傳), Liu Chuang-su-kung tsou-i 劉壯肅公奏議 (Memorials of Liu Ming-ch'uan), 22 chüan (preface dated 1906).

Liu P'an-sui 劉盼遂, "Liang Jen-kung hsien-sheng chuan" 梁任公先生傳 (A biography of Liang Ch'i-ch'ao) T'u-shu-kuan-hsueh chi-k'an 圖書館學季刊, 3. 1-2: 135-137 (1929).

Liu Ping-li 劉炳瓈, Kuo-fu ssu-hsiang t'i-hsi shu-yao 國父思想體系述要 (An account of essential points of Sun Yat-sen's system of thinking; Shanghai, 1946), 98 pp.

Liu Yueh-yun 劉嶽雲, Shih-chiu-te-chai tsa-chu 食舊惠齋雜著 (Miscellaneous writings of Liu Yueh-yun), 4 ts'e (1882).

Liu Yueh-yun 劉嶽雲, "Ko-wu chung fa hsü" 格物中法叙 (Preface to Ko-wu chung fa), in Shih-chiu-te-chai tsa-chu, ts'e 1.

Lo Erh-kang 羅爾綱, "Ming-wang hou Han-tsu ti tzu-chueh ho mi-mi chieh-she" 明亡後漢族的自覺和秘密結社 (Chinese national awakening and secret organizations after the fall of the Ming dynasty), Tientsin I-shih-pao: "Shih-hsueh" 史學 (History supplement), no. 1 (April 30, 1935).

Lo Erh-kang 羅爾綱, T'ai-p'ing T'ien-kuo shih-kang 太平天國史綱 (Outline history of the Taiping rebellion; Shanghai: Commercial Press, 1937), 134 pp.

Lo Erh-kang, T'ai-p'ing T'ien-kuo shih-kao 太平天國史稿 (A draft history of the Taiping rebellion; Peking: K'ai-ming shu-tien, 1951), 5 & 285 pp.

Lo Erh-kang 羅爾綱, T'ai-p'ing T'ien-kuo shih ts'ung-k'ao 太平天國史叢考 (Miscellaneous studies on the history of the Taiping rebellion; Shanghai: Cheng-chung shu-chü, 1943; 2nd. printing, 1947), 196 pp.

Lo Erh-kang 羅爾綱, T'ien-ti-hui wen-hsien lu 天地會文獻錄 (Documents of the Heaven and Earth Society; (Cheng-chung shu-chü, 1943).

Lo Hsiang-lin 羅香林, Kuo-fu chih ta-hsueh shih-tai 國父之大學時代 (The college years of the father of our nation; Chungking: Tu-li ch'u-pan-she, 1945), 164 pp.

Lo Hsiang-lin 羅香林, "Ya-p'ien chan-cheng Yueh-tung i-min k'ang-Ying shih-liao hsü-lu" 鴉片戰爭粵東義民抗英史料叙錄 (Copies of historical materials concerning the anti-British movement among the people of Kwangtung during the Opium War), She-hui k'o-hsueh ts'ung-k'an 社會科學叢刊 ("Studies in Social Sciences"), National Central University, Nanking, 2.2: 145-164 (January 1936).

Lo Wen-kan, "China's Introduction of Foreign Systems," CSPSR 8.4: 172-182 (October 1924).

Lou T'ung-sun 樓桐孫, San-min chu-i yen-chiu 三民主義研究 (A study of San-min chu-i; Shanghai: Commercial Press, no date [1934?]), 222 pp.

Lu Hsi-ta 魯昔達, "Tseng Tso hsiang-wu chi ch'i-t'a" 曾左相惡及其他 (The disagreement between Tseng and Tso and other matters), Ku-chin, no. 32: 28-32 (October 1943).

Lü-li yuan-yuan 律曆淵源 (Compendium on the calendar, music and mathematics), compiled under imperial auspices 1723-1756, including three works: Li-hsiang k'ao-ch'eng 歷象考成, 42 chüan, on the calendar; Shu-li ching-yun 數理精蘊, 53 chüan, on mathematics; and Lü-lü cheng-i 律呂正義, 5 chüan, on music.

Lü Liu-liang 呂留良, Lü Yung-hui wen-chi 呂用晦文集 (Collected essays of Lü Liu-liang), in Kuo-ts'ui ts'ung-shu 國粹叢書, ts'e 5-6.

Ma Chien-chung 馬建忠, Shih-k'o-chai chi-yen 適可齋記言 (Notes from the Shih-k'o-chai studio), in Hsi-cheng ts'ung-shu, ts'e 27 (preface dated 1896).

Ma Feng-chen 馬奉琛, Ch'ing-tai hsing-cheng chih-tu yen-chiu ts'an-k'ao shu-mu 清代行政制度研究參攷書目 (Bibliography for research on the administrative system of the Ch'ing dynasty; Peiping: Peking University Press, 1935), 228 pp.

MacNair, H. F., Modern Chinese History: Selected Readings (Shanghai: Commercial Press, 1923), 910 pp.

Mai Chien-tseng 麥健曾 and Li Ying-chao 李應兆, Chung-kuo t'ieh-tao wen-t'i ts'an-k'ao tzu-liao so-yin 中國鐵道問題參考資料索引 (An index to reference material on Chinese railroad problems; Peiping: Peiping branch of the Research Institute of Chiao-t'ung University, 1936).

Mai Chung-hua 麥仲華, comp., Huang-ch'ao ching-shih wen hsin-pien 皇朝經世文新編 (New supplement to the Huang-ch'ao ching-shih wen-pien), 21 chüan (Shanghai: Shang-hai shu-chü, 1901).

Makino Kyōji 牧野京次, "Ri Kō-shō no denki" 李鴻章の傳記 (Biography of Li Hung-chang), Shusho geppo 收書月報, no. 65.

Malone, C. B., History of the Peking Summer Palaces (Urbana, Ill.,1934), 247 pp.

Mantetsu Chōsa Kyoku 滿鐵調查局 (South Manchurian Railway Research Bureau), Shina kōsan shigen bunken mokuroku 支那礦產資源文獻目錄 (A bibliography of literature on Chinese natural resources; Tōkyō, 1943), 88 pp.

Martin, W. A. P., trans., Wan-kuo kung-fa 萬國公法 (Wheaton's International Law), 4 chüan (Peking, 1864).

Martin, W. A. P., A Cycle of Cathay (New York, second edition, 1896), 464 pp.

Martin, W. A. P., The Lore of Cathay; or The Intellect of China (New York, 1901), 480 pp.

Matsumoto Sumio 松本純郎, Mito gaku no genryū 水戶學の源流 (The origin of the Mito school; Tōkyō: Chō-sō shoten, 1945), 314 pp.

Maybon, Albert, La Politique Chinoise, étude sur les doctrines des partis en Chine, 1898-1908 (Paris, 1908), 268 pp.

McCall, Davy H., "Chang Chien-mandarin turned manufacturer," Papers On China, 2: 93-102 (May 1948).

McCall, Davy H., "Chang Chien and the establishment of the Tungchow cotton mills," unpublished paper (1948) on file in the Harvard Chinese Library, Regional Studies collection.

Mei Ying 梅影, "Wu-hsü cheng-pien chen-wen" 戊戌政變珍聞 (Valuable information on the reform movement of 1898), Jen-wen 人文, 7.10: 1-6 (December 1936).

Meijer, Marinus Johan, The Introduction of Modern Criminal Law in China, Sinica Indonesiana, Vol. II. (Batavia: De Unie, 1950), 212 pp.

Men-se t'an-hu-k'o 捫蝨談虎客 (pseud.), Chin-shih Chung-kuo mi-shih 近世中國秘史 (A "confidential" modern Chinese history), 2 vols. (Shanghai, 1905).

Mencius, see Meng-tzu chu-su.

Meng Ch'i 孟祁, "Chi Ku Hung-ming weng" 記辜鴻銘翁 (On Mr. Ku Hung-ming), Jen-chien shih, no. 12: 44-45 (September 1934).

Meng Ssu-ming, "The Organization and Functions of the Tsungli Yamen"(Harvard Ph.D. Thesis, 1949) 188 pp.

Meng-tzu chu-su 孟子注疏 (The works of Mencius), in Shih-san-ching chu-su, ts'e 155-160.

Michie, Alexander, The Englishman in China during the Victorian Era, 2 vols. (Edinburgh, 1910).

Mikami,Yoshio, Development of Mathematics in China and Japan (Leipzig, 1913), 347 pp.

Min Erh-ch'ang 閔爾昌, ed., Pei-chuan-chi pu 碑傳集補 (Supplement to the Pei-chuan-chi), 60 chüan (Peiping: Yenching University, 1931).

Momose Hiromu 百瀬弘 , "Fū Kei-fun to sono chojutsu ni tsuite" 馮桂芬と其の著述に就いて (On Feng Kuei-fen and his writings), Tōa ronsō 東亞論叢 2: 95-122 (January 1940). Translated into Chinese in a condensed form in Chung-ho yueh-k'an 中和月刊 , 3.3: 53-66 (March 1942).

Morse, H. B., International Relations of the Chinese Empire, 3 vols. (London, 1910-1918).

Mu Hsiang-yueh 穆湘玥 , "Chung-kuo mien-chih-yeh fa-ta-shih" 中國棉織發達史 (Progress of China's cotton textile industry for the past 50 years), in Tsui-chin chih wu-shih-nien, pp. 1-5 (in the middle of the volume, which is not paged consecutively).

Mu Hsiang-yueh 穆湘玥 , Ou-ch'u ssu-shih tzu-shu 藕初四十自述 (Autobiography at forty by Mu Hsiang-yueh; Shanghai: Commercial Press, 1926), 94+226+81 pp.

Murakami Tomoyuki 村上知行 , Bojutsu seihen shiwa 戊戌政變史話 (Historical accounts of the coup d'état of 1898; Peking: Hsin-min yin-shu-kuan, 1944), 244 pp.

Murphey, Rhoads, Shanghai, Key to Modern China (Cambridge: Harvard University Press, 1953), 232 pp.

Nelson, William E., "One-party government in China," Far Eastern Survey, 17.10: 118-121 (May 19, 1948).

Niida Noboru 仁井田陞 ed., et al., Kindai Chūgoku kenkyū 近代中國研究 (Researches on modern China; Tōkyō: Kōgakusha, 1948), 361 pp.

Nishida Tamotsu 西田保 , Sa Sō-dō to Shin-kyō mondai 左宗棠ト新疆問題 (Tso Tsung-t'ang and the problem of Sinkiang; Tōkyō: Hakubunkan, 1942).

Nolde, John J., "The "Canton Question," 1842-1849: A Preliminary Investigation into Chinese Anti-foreignism and its Effect upon China's Diplomatic Relations with the West" (Ph.D. dissertation, Cornell University, 1950), 271 pp.

Norman, E. Herbert, Japan's Emergence as a Modern State (New York: Institute of Pacific Relations, 1940), 254 pp.

North China Herald, Shanghai, weekly, 1850—

Nü-shih hsueh-yuan ch'i-k'an 女師學院期刊 (Journal of the Hopei Teachers' College for Women), Tientsin, beginning 1933, semi-annually.

Odontines, L., "Chang Chih-tung and the Reform Movement in China," translated from the German by E. Zillig, The East of Asia, 1.1: 19-42 (1902).

Ojima Sukema 小島祐馬 Chūgoku no kakumei shisō 中國の革命思想、 (Chinese revolutionary thought; Tōkyō: Kōbundō, 1952), 166 pp.

Ono Noriaki 小野則秋 , Son Bun 孫文 (Sun Yat-sen; Tōkyō: Daigadō, 1948), 257 pp.

Onogawa Hidemi 小野川秀美 , "Shimmatsu hempōron no seiritsu" 清末變法論の成立 ("The Formation of the Reformatory Thought at the End of the Ts'ing Dynasty"), Tōhō gakuhō 東方學報 , Kyōto, 20: 153-184 (March 1951).

Onogawa Hidemi 小野川秀美 , "Shimmatsu yōmuha no undō" 清末洋務派の運動 ("On the Movement of Europeanizing at the End of the Ch'ing Era"), Tōyōshi kenkyū ("The Journal of Oriental Researches"), 10.6: 429-466 (February 1950).

Onogawa Hidemi 小野川秀美 , "Shimmatsu no shisō to shinkaron" 清末の思想と進化論 ("Political Thoughts and the Evolutionary Theory at the End of the Tsing 清 Dynasty"), Tōhō gakuhō 東方學報 , Kyōto, 21: 1-36 (March 1952).

Otake Fumio 小竹文夫, "Mimmatsu irai seisho kō" 明末以來西書考 (A study of Western books published in Chinese since the late Ming period), Shina kenkyū 支那研究 43: 35-71 (January 1937).

Ou-yang Yü-ch'ien 歐陽予倩, comp., T'an Ssu-t'ung shu-chien 譚嗣同書簡 (Letters of T'an Ssu-t'ung; Shanghai: Wen-hua kung-ying she, 1948), 138 pp.

Overdijkink, G. W., Lin Tse-hsǔ, (Leiden: E. J. Brill, 1938), 173 pp.

Owen, D. E., British Opium Policy in China and India (New Haven: Yale University Press, 1934), 399 pp.

Pan Ku 班固, Ch'ien-Han shu 前漢書 (History of the Former Han), 120 chǔan (Shanghai, T'ung-wen shu-chǔ edition).

P'an Kung-chan 潘公展, Wu-shih-nien-lai ti Chung-kuo 五十年來的中國 (China in the past fifty years; Chungking: Sheng-li ch'u-pan-she, 1945), 339 pp.

P'an Wei-tung, The Chinese Constitution; a study of forty years of constitution-making in China (Washington: The Catholic University of America Press, 1945), 327 pp.

Papers on China, from the Regional Studies Seminars, mimeographed for private distribution by the Committee on International and Regional Studies, Harvard University, Cambridge: 1 (December 1947), 2 (May 1948), 3 (May 1949), 4 (April 1950), 5 (May 1951), 6 (March 1952), 7 (February 1953).

Papers Relating to Foreign Affairs, 1867 (Washington D. C., 1868).

Parker, E. H. (tr.), "The Published Letters of the Senior Marquis Tseng," China Review, 18.6: 347-365 (May-June 1890).

Peake, Cyrus H., "Some aspects of the introduction of modern science into China," Isis, 63: 173-219 (December 1934).

Pei-yang hai-chǔn chang-ch'eng 北洋海軍章程 (Regulations of the Pei-yang Navy), compiled by Chung-kuo tsung-li hai-chǔn ya-men, 2 ts'e (Tientsin, 1888).

Pelliot, Paul, review of The Hung Society or the Society of Heaven and Earth, par J. S. M. Ward et W. G. Stirling, T'oung-pao XXV, 444-48 (Leide, 1928).

P'eng Tse-i 彭澤益, "Chang Chien ti ssu-hsiang chi ch'i shih-yeh" 張謇的思想及其事業 (Chang Chien's ideas and career), Tung-fang tsa-chih, 40.14: 54-60 (1944).

Pfister, Louis, S. J., Notices biographiques et bibliographiques sur les Jésuites de l'ancienne Mission de Chine (1552-1773), 2 vols. (Shanghai: Variétés sinologiques, nos. 59-60, 1932, 1934).

Powell, Ralph L., "The rise of Yuan Shih-k'ai and the Pei-yang Army," Papers on China, 3: 225-256 (1949).

Prince Kung 恭親王 (I-hsin 奕訢), Lo-tao-t'ang shih-wen ch'ao 樂道堂詩文鈔 (Reproduction of I-hsin's poems and essays), 12 ts'e (block-print edition, 1867).

Pritchard, Earl H., Anglo-Chinese Relations during the Seventeenth and Eighteenth Centuries (Urbana: The University of Illinois Press, 1929), 244 pp.

Pritchard, Earl H., "The Kotow in the Macartney Embassy to China of 1793," Far Eastern Quarterly, 2.2: 163-203 (February 1943).

Rawlinson, John L., "The Lay-Osborn Flotilla: Its Development and Significance," Papers on China 4:58-73 (1950).

(Reform movement), "Kuan-yü wu-hsü cheng-pien hsin shih-liao" 關於戊戌政變新史料 (New historical material concerning the reform movement of 1898), Ta-kung-pao, shih-ti chou-k'an 大公報史地周刊 , 4.95 (July 1936).

(Reform movement), "Lun pien-fa chih ching-shen" 論變法之精神 (On the spirit of reform), Tung-fang tsa-chih, no. 7: 142-144 (1904).

Rosso, Antonio Sisto, O. F. M., Apostolic Legations to China of the eighteenth century (South Pasadena: P. D. and Ione Perkins, 1948), 502 pp.

Rowbotham, Arnold H., Missionary and Mandarin: the Jesuits at the Court of China (Berkeley: University of California Press, 1942), 374 pp.

Saeki Yoshirō 佐伯好郎 , Shinchō Kirisuto-kyō no kenkyū 清朝基督敎の研究 (A study of Christianity under the Ch'ing Dynasty; Tōkyō: Shunjūsha 春秋社 , 1949), 640 + 24 pp.

Sakai, Robert K., "Ts'ai Yuan-p'ei as a synthesizer of Western and Chinese thought," Papers on China, Cambridge, 3: 170-192 (May 1949).

Sanetō Keishū 實藤惠秀 , Chūgokujin Nippon ryūgaku shikō 中國人日本留學史稿 (Draft history of Chinese students in Japan; Tōkyō: Nikka gakkai 日華學會 , 1939), 368 pp., illus.

Sanetō Keishū 實藤惠秀 , Kindai Nisshi bunka ron 近代日支文化論 (On modern Sino-Japanese culture), Tōkyō: Daitō 大東 , 1941, 269 pp., illus.

Sanetō, Keishū 實藤惠秀 , "Kindai Shina to gairai shisō" 近代支那と外來思想 , in Kindai Shina shisō 近代支那思想, pp. 143-176 (Tōkyō: Kōfūkan, 1942).

Sanetō Keishū 實藤惠秀 , Meiji Nisshi bunka kōshō 明治日支文化交涉 (Sino-Japanese cultural relations in the Meiji period; Tōkyō: Kōfūkan 光風館 , 1943), 394 pp., illus.

Sanetō Keishū 實藤惠秀 , "Wang T'ao ti tu-Jih ho Jih-pen wen-jen" 王韜的渡日和日本文人 (Wang T'ao's trip to Japan and Japanese scholars), tr. by Chang Ming-san 張銘三 , in Jih-pen yen-chiu 日本研究 , 3.6: 27-39 (1944).

Sano Kesami 佐野袈裟美 , Shina kindai hyakunenshi 支那近代百年史 (History of China in the past hundred years), 2 vols. (Tōkyō: Hakuyōsha, 1939-40).

Sansom, Sir G. B., Japan, A Short Cultural History, revised edition (New York: D. Appleton-Century Co., 1943), 554 pp.

Sansom, Sir G. B., The Western World and Japan (New York: Alfred A. Knopf, 1950), 504 pp.

Schwartz, Benjamin, "Ch'en Tu-hsiu, his pre-Communist phase," Papers on China, 2: 167-197 (1948).

Schwartz, Benjamin, "Ch'en Tu-hsiu and the acceptance of the modern West," Journal of the History of Ideas, 12.1: 61-74 (January 1951).

Schwartz, Benjamin I., Chinese Communism and the Rise of Mao (Cambridge: Harvard University Press, 1951), 258 pp.

Shang-hai-shih t'ung-chih-kuan ch'i-k'an 上海市通志館期刊 (A periodical publication of the Shanghai Gazeteer Office), no. 2 (1933), 513 pp.

Shang Ping-ho 尚東和 , "Yuan ta-tsung-t'ung lueh-shih" 袁大總統略史 (A brief history of President Yuan), ch. 34 in Hsin-jen ch'un-ch'iu 辛壬春秋 (A chronicle of 1911-1912), 16 ts'e (block-print edition of 1924).

Shang-shu cheng-i 尚書正義 (The Book of History), in Shih-san-ching chu-su, ts'e 5-12.

Sharman, Lyon, Sun Yat Sen, his life and its meaning, a critical biography (New York: John Day, 1934), 418 pp.

She-hui-hsueh chieh 社會學界 (The sociological world), published by Yenching University, Department of Sociology, Peiping, beginning 1927, annual.

Sheeks, Robert, "A re-examination of the I-ho Ch'üan and its role in the Boxer Movement," Papers on China, 1: 74-135 (1947).

Shen Chien 沈鑑, "Ssu-shih-yü-nien ch'ien chih lien-E wai-chiao" 四十餘年前之聯俄外交 (The pro-Russian foreign policy [of China] some forty years ago), Chung-kuo wen-hua yen-chiu-so hui-k'an 中國文化研究所彙刊, vol. 2: 151-184 (1942).

Shen Ch'un 沈純, Hsi-shih li-ts'e 西事蠡測 (A glimpse into Western affairs), in Hsiao-fang-hu-chai yü-ti ts'ung-ch'ao, ts'e 62.

Shen-pao-kuan 申報館, comp., Tsui-chin chih wu-shih-nien, Shen-pao-kuan wu-shih chou-nien chi-nien 最近之五十年,申報館五十週年紀念 (The past fifty years, in commemoration of the Shen-pao's Golden Jubilee, 1872-1922), a special supplement published by the Shen-pao (Shanghai, 1923).

Shen-pao nien-chien 申報年鑑 (The Shen-pao year book), first issue, edited by Chang Tzu-sheng 張梓生 and others, 1 ts'e (Shanghai, 1933).

Shen Tsu-hsien 沈祖憲 ed., Yang-shou-yuan tsou-i chi-yao 養壽園奏議輯要 (A collection of important memorials of Yang-shou-yuan [Yuan Shih-k'ai]), block-print edition (publisher and date unknown).

Shen Tsu-hsien 沈祖憲 and Wu K'ai-sheng 吳闓生, Jung-an ti-tzu chi 容菴弟子記 (An account of Jung-an [Yuan Shih-k'ai] by his disciples; publisher unknown, 1913).

Shen T'ung-sheng 沈桐生, ed., Kuang-hsü cheng-yao 光緒政要 (Important documents concerning the Kuang-hsü administration), 30 ts'e (Shanghai: Nan-yang kuan-shu-chü, 1908).

Sheng Hsuan-huai 盛宣懷, Yü-chai ts'un-kao 愚齋存稿 (Extant writings of Sheng Hsuan-huai), 100 chüan (Shanghai: published by Ssu-pu lou, 1939).

Sheng K'ang 盛康, Huang-ch'ao ching-shih-wen hsü-pien 皇朝經世文續編 (Supplement to the Huang-ch'ao ching-shih wen-pien), 80 chüan, 10 ts'e (1897 edition).

Shih-liao hsun-k'an 史料旬刊 (Historical materials published thrice monthly) 40 volumes (Peking: Palace Museum 1930-31).

Shih, Vincent Yu-chung, "Interpretations of the Taiping Tien-kuo by Noncommunist Chinese Writers," Far Eastern Quarterly 10.3: 248-257 (May 1951).

Shina kōsan shigen bunken mokuroku, see Mantetsu Chōsa Kyoku.

Shu An 銖庵, "Hsiang-hsiang Tseng-shih i-wen" 湘鄉曾氏遺聞 (Anecdotes of the Tseng family of Hsiang-hsiang), Jen-chien-shih, no. 26: 9-13 (April 1935).

Shu Hsin-ch'eng 舒新城 ed., Chin-tai Chung-kuo chiao-yü shih-liao 近代中國教育史料 (Historial materials on modern Chinese education), in Chiao-yü ts'ung-shu 教育叢書 (Education series), 4 vols. (Shanghai, 1923), pp. 339+264+245+198+39.

Shu Hsin-ch'eng 舒新城, Chin-tai Chung-kuo liu-hsueh shih 近代中國留學史 (History of education of students abroad in modern China; Shanghai: Chiao-yü ts'ung-shu, 1927), 300 pp.

Shun Pao, see Shen-pao.

Shuo-wen yueh-k'an 說文月刊, published in Shanghai and Chungking, beginning 1939.

So Kwan-wai (Su Chun-wei 蘇均煒), "Western Influence and the Chinese Reform Movement of 1898," (Ph.D. dissertation, University of Wisconsin, 1950), 269 pp.

Soothill, W. E., Timothy Richard of China (London: Seeley & Co., 1924), 330 pp.

South Manchurian Railway, see Mantetsu Chōsa Kyoku.

Ssu-chou chih 四洲志 (Gazetteer of the four continents), in Hsiao-fang-hu-chai yü-ti ts'ung-ch'ao, ts'e 82.

Ssu-k'u ch'üan-shu 四庫全書 (Complete library in four branches of literature), compiled between 1773 and 1782 under the patronage of Emperor Ch'ien-lung, 3450 titles.

Ssu-k'u ch'üan-shu tsung-mu t'i-yao 四庫全書總目提要 (An annotated bibliography of books in the Ssu-k'u ch'üan-shu), 200 chüan, compiled by Chi Yun and others in 1782, Tai-tung shu-chü edition.

Ssu-luan 嗣鑾, "Ku Hung-ming tsai Te-kuo" 辜鴻銘在德國 (Ku Hung-ming in Germany), Jen-chien-shih, no. 12: 40-41 (September 1934).

Ssu-ma Ch'ien 司馬遷, Shih-chi 史記, 130 chüan, in Erh-shih-ssu shih, T'ung-wen-shu-chü edition (1894), ts'e 1-26.

Ssu-ma Kuang 司馬光, Tzu-chih t'ung-chien 資治通鑑 (Comprehensive mirror for aid in government), 294 chüan, 100 ts'e.

Stanley, C. J., "Hu Kuang-yung and China's Early Foreign Loans" (Ph.D. dissertation, Harvard University, 1951), 164 pp.

Steiger, G. N., China and the Occident (New Haven: Yale University Press, 1927), 349 pp.

Su Ch'eng-chien 蘇誠鑑, "Li Hung-chang i-kuan ti fan-Jih cheng-ts'e" 李鴻章一貫的反日政策 (Li Hung-chang's consistent anti-Japanese policy), Hsin cheng-chih 新政治, 3.5: 76-82 (1940).

Su Ch'ih 素癡 (Chang Yin-lin 張蔭麟), "Chin-tai Chung-kuo hsueh-shu-shih shang chih Liang Jen-kung" 近代中國學術史上之梁任公 (Liang Ch'i-ch'ao in the history of modern Chinese learning), in the Literary Supplement of the Tientsin Ta-kung-pao 大公報文學副刊, Feb. 11, 1929.

Su Yü 蘇輿, I-chiao ts'ung-pien 翼教叢編 (A collection of documents for the protection of Confucian teaching; 1898).

Suan-ching shih-shu 算經十書 (Ten textbooks on mathematics), 1773 edition. Compiled by K'ung Chi-han 孔繼涵, including nine of the original works of 1084 of the same title, one ancient mathematical treatise, Tai Chen's Ts'e-suan 戴震策算, and Kou-ku ko-yuan chi 勾股割圜記, 3 chüan.

Sun, E-tu Zen, "The Chinese Constitutional Missions of 1905-1906," Journal of Modern History, 24.3: 251-268 (September 1952).

Sun Hao 孫灝, Hai-kuo t'u-chih cheng-shih 海國圖志徵實 (Errata and Supplements to the Hai-kuo t'u-chih), 20 ts'e (Shanghai, 1902).

Sun Yat-sen 孫逸仙, Chung-shan ch'üan-shu 中山全書 (Complete works of Sun Yat-sen), 4 vols. (Shanghai: Ta-hua shu-chü, 1927).

Sun Yat-sen 孫逸仙, "Neng-chih pi neng-hsing" 能知必能行 (Whatever can be known can certainly be carried out), ch. 6 of Sun Wen hsueh-shuo 孫文學說, in Chung-shan ch'üan-shu.

Sun Yat-sen 孫逸仙, "T'ung-meng-hui hsuan-yen" 同盟會宣言 (Manifesto of the T'ung-meng-hui), in Chung-shan ch'üan-shu, vol. 4, 1-4.

Sun Yat-sen 孫逸仙, Tsung-li ch'üan-chi 總理全集 (Complete collected works of the Director-General), edited by Hu Han-min 胡漢民, 4 chi in 5 vols. (Shanghai: Min-chih shu-chü, 1930).

Sung Ying-hsing 宋應星, T'ien-kung k'ai-wu 天工開物 (Natural resources utilized for manufacturing; first printed, 1637; T'ao Hsiang 陶湘 edition, 1927).

Tabohashi Kiyoshi 田保橋潔, "Giwakempiran to Nichi-Ro" 義和拳匪亂と日露 (The Boxer Rebellion and Japan and Russia), pp. 1051-1106 in Tōzai kōshō shiron 東西交渉史論 (Treatises on the history of East-West relations), 2 vols. (Tōkyō: Fuzambō 富山房, 1939), 1410 pp.

Tabohashi Kiyoshi 田保橋潔, Nisshin seneki gaikōshi no kenkyū 日清戰役外交史の研究 ("A Diplomatic History of the Sino-Japanese War 1894-1895"; Tōkyō: Tokō 刀江, 1951), 556 pp.; English summary, 5 pp.

Ta-Ch'ing Kuang-hsü hsin fa-ling 大清光緒新法令 (New laws and ordinances of the Kuang-hsü reign), 20 ts'e (Shanghai: compiled by the Commercial Press, 1909).

Ta-Ch'ing lü-li 大清律例 (Laws and precedents of the Ch'ing dynasty), 47 + 5 chüan (incomplete) in 26 ts'e (revised edition, 1870).

Ta-i chüeh-mi lu 大義覺迷錄 (Record of the awakening of the misled by grand principles), 4 chüan (printed, 1730).

Tai Chin-hsieo, "The Life and Work of Ts'ai Yuan-p'ei" (Ed. D. dissertation, Harvard School of Education, 1952).

Tai Hung-tz'u 戴鴻慈, Ch'u-shih chiu-kuo jih-chi 出使九國日記 (Diary on diplomatic missions to nine countries; Peking: Ti-i shu-chü, 1906), 334 pp.

Tai Hung-tz'u 戴鴻慈 and Tuan-fang 端方, ed., Ou-Mei cheng-chih yao-i 歐美政治要義 (Essentials of political administration in Europe and America), 4 ts'e (lithographic edition, 1907).

T'ai-hsü 釋太虛, Jen-sheng-kuan ti k'o-hsueh 人生觀的科學 (A science of the philosophy of life; Shanghai: T'ai-tung Book Co., 1925).

T'ai-p'ing T'ien-kuo wen-shu 太平天國文書 (Collection of letters by Taiping leaders; Peiping: photolithographic copy of 1933).

T'ai-p'ing T'ien-kuo ko-ming yun-tung lun-wen chi 太平天國革命運動論文集 (Symposium on the T'ai-p'ing Revolutionary Movement), edited by the Institute of Historical Research of North China University (Hua-pei ta-hsueh li-shih yen-chiu shih; Peking: San-lien, 1950), 165 p.

Tamagna, Frank M., Banking and Finance in China (New York: Institute of Pacific Relations, 1942), 400 pp.

T'an Ssu-t'ung 譚嗣同, Jen-hsueh 仁學 (A study of benevolence), in Ch'ing-i-pao ch'üan-pien 清議報全編, the second collection, A, ts'e 3.

T'an Ssu-t'ung 譚嗣同, T'an Liu-yang ch'üan-chi 譚瀏陽全集 (Complete works of T'an Ssu-t'ung), including nien-p'u 年譜, 8 + 1 chüan (published 1925).

T'ang Chen 湯震, Wei-yen 危言 (Warnings), 4 chüan (Shanghai, 1890).

T'ang Chi-ch'ing 唐際清, "E tsu Lü-shun Ta-lien shih Li Hung-chang shou-hui chih cheng-chü" 俄租旅順大連時李鴻章受賄之證據 (Evidences of Li Hung-chang's bribery when Port Author and Dairen were leased to Russia), Nan-k'ai chou-k'an 南開週刊, no. 48.

T'ang Ch'ing-tseng 唐慶增, "Tseng Kuo-fan chih ching-chi ssu-hsiang" 曾國藩之經濟思想 (Tseng Kuo-fan's economic ideas), Ching-chi-hsueh chi-k'an 經濟學季刊, 5.4: 52-60 (1935).

T'ang Hsiang-lung 湯象龍, "Min-kuo i-ch'ien kuan-shui tan-pao chih wai-chai" 民國以前關稅担保之外債 (The foreign loans secured on the customs revenue before 1911), Chung-kuo chin-tai ching-chi-shih yen-chiu chi-k'an, 3.1: 3-8 (1935).

T'ang Leang-li, The Foundations of Modern China (London: N. Douglas, 1928), 290 pp.

Tao, L. K., "A Chinese Political Theorist [Huang Tsung-hsi] of the 17th Century," CSPSR, 2.1: 71-82 (March 1917).

T'ao K'ang-te 陶亢德, comp., Tzu-chuan chih i-chang 自傳之一章 (A collection of autobiographies; Shanghai: Yü-chou-feng she, 1938), 198 pp.

Teng Ssu-yü 鄧嗣禹, Chung-kuo k'ao-shih chih-tu shih 中國考試制度史 (A history of the Chinese civil service examination system; Nanking: The Examination Yuan, 1936).

Teng Ssu-yü, Chang Hsi and the Treaty of Nanking, 1842 (Chicago: University of Chicago Press, 1944), 191 pp.

Teng, Ssu-yü, New Light on the History of the Taiping Rebellion (Cambridge: Harvard University Press, 1950), 132 pp.

Teng Ssu-yü and Knight Biggerstaff, An Annotated Bibliography of Selected Chinese Reference Works, revised edition (Cambridge: Harvard University Press, 1950), 326 pp. See also under Fairbank.

Teng Yü-han 鄧玉函 (Terrenz), and Wang Cheng 王徵, ed. and tr., Yuan-Hsi ch'i-ch'i t'u-shuo lu-tsui 遠西奇器圖說錄最 (European works on mechanical principles, with illustrations), commonly known as Ch'i-ch'i t'u-shuo, 3 chüan (printed in Peking, 1627). Edition of Shou-shan-ko ts'ung-shu 守山閣叢書, 3 chüan (1833).

Tewksbury, Donald G., Source Book on Far Eastern Political Ideologies, Modern period, China-Japan, preliminary edition (New York: Teachers College, Columbia University, 1949), 189 pp.

Tezuka Masao 手塚正夫, Shina jūkōgyō hattatsu shi 支那重工業發達史 (History of the development of Chinese heavy industry; Tōkyō, 1944), 19+548+14 pp.

Ting Chih-p'ing 丁致聘, Chung-kuo chin ch'i-shih-nien-lai chiao-yü chi-shih 中國近七十年來教育紀事 (Events in Chinese education during the last seventy years; Shanghai: published by Kuo-li pien-i kuan 國立編輯館 [National Institute of Compilation and Translation], 1935), 291 pp.

Ting Tse-liang 丁則良, Li T'i-mo-t'ai 李提摩太 (Timothy Richard; Peking: K'ai ming Book Co., 1951), 66 pp.

Ting Wen-chiang (V. K. Ting) 丁文江, "Wu-shih-nien-lai Chung-kuo chih k'uang-yeh" 五十年來中國之礦業 (China's mining industry for the past 50 years), in Tsui-chin chih wu-shih-nien, pp. 1-14.

Tobar, Jerome, Chang Chih-tung, K'iuen-hio p'ien; exhortations à l'étude, Variétés Sinologiques, no. 26 (Chang-hai, 1909).

T'oung-pao 通報 Archives pour servir à l'étude de l'histoire, des langues, de la Géographie et de l'ethnographie de l'Asia Orientale, ed. by Gustave Schlegel et Henri Cordier, et al. (Leiden: E. J. Brill, 1890-   ).

Tsai-tse 戴澤, K'ao-ch'a cheng-chih jih-chi 考察政治日記 (Diary of political studies [abroad]; Peking, 1908), 136 pp.

Ts'ai Shang-ssu 蔡尚思, "T'an Ssu-t'ung hsueh-shu ssu-hsiang t'i-yao" 譚嗣同學術思想提要 (An outline of T'an Ssu-t'ung's academic ideas), Chung-kuo chien-she, 4.2: 49-53 (May 1947).

Ts'ai Yuan-p'ei 蔡元培, Ts'ai Chieh-min hsien-sheng yen-hsing lu 蔡孑民先生言行錄 (A record of the words and actions of Ts'ai Yuan-p'ei; Peking: Peking University, 1920), 580 pp.

Ts'ai Yuan-p'ei, "The development of Chinese education," Asiatic Review, vol. 20: 499-509 (1924).

Ts'ai Yuan-p'ei 蔡元培, Chung-kuo lun-li-hsueh shih 中國倫理學史 (A history of Chinese ethics; Shanghai: Commercial Press, 1937), 151 pp.

Ts'ai Yuan-p'ei 蔡元培, "Wo tsai chiao-yü-chieh ti ching-yen" 我在教育界的經驗 (My experiences in the educational field), in T'ao K'ang-te, Tzu-chuan chih i-chang, pp. 1-12.

Ts'ai Yuan-p'ei 蔡元培, "Wu-shih-nien-lai Chung-kuo chih che-hsueh" 五十年來中國之哲學 (Chinese philosophical studies in the past fifty years), in Shen-pao-kuan, Tsui-chin chih wu-shih-nien, pp. 1-10.

Ts'ai Yuan-p'ei 蔡元培, "Chui-tao Ts'ai Chieh-min hsien-sheng t'e-chi" 追悼蔡孑民先生特輯 (Special memorial issue on Ts'ai Yuan-p'ei), Tung-fang tsa-chih, 37.8 (1940).

Ts'ai Yuan-p'ei 蔡元培, Yü-chou feng 宇宙風, no. 24 (1940), memorial issue on Ts'ai Yuan-p'ei.

Tsao Wen-yen, The Constitutional Structure of Modern China (Melbourne: Melbourne Press, 1947), 304 pp.

Tseng Chi-tse 曾紀澤, Tseng Hui-min-kung shih-Hsi jih-chi 曾惠敏公使西日記 (Diary of Marquis Tseng's mission to the West), printed in 2 chüan in Tseng Hui-min-kung i-chi, and reprinted under the title Shih-Hsi jih-chi in Hsiao-fang-hu-chai yü-ti ts'ung-ch'ao, ts'e 78. See also ts'e 58 of the latter work, entitled Ch'u-shih Ying-Fa jih-chi 出使英法日記 (Diary of a mission to England and France).

Tseng Chi-tse 曾紀澤, Chin-yao ch'ou-pi 金軺籌筆 (Records of an imperial mission), first printed in 1887, in I-hsiu-shan-fang ts'ung-shu 挹秀山房叢書, ts'e 17-20.

Tseng Chi-tse 曾紀澤, Tseng Hui-min-kung i-chi 曾惠敏公遺集 (Collected works of Tseng Chi-tse), 17 chüan (Shanghai, 1893).

Tseng K'un-hua 曾錕化, Chung-kuo t'ieh-lu shih 中國鐵路史 (History of Chinese railways; Peking, 1924), 954 pp.

Tseng Kuo-fan 曾國藩, Tseng Wen-cheng-kung ch'üan-chi 曾文正公全集 (Complete works of Tseng Kuo-fan), 174 chüan (1876).

Tseng Kuo-fan 曾國藩, Tseng Wen-cheng-kung nien-p'u 曾文正公年譜 (A chronological biography of Tseng Kuo-fan), comp. by Li Shu-ch'ang 黎庶昌 and others, 12 chüan, in Tseng Wen-cheng-kung ch'üan-chi, ts'e 33-36.

Tseng Kuo-fan 曾國藩, Tseng Wen-cheng-kung shou-shu jih-chi 曾文正公手書日記 (Autographic diary of Tseng Kuo fan [from 1841-1871]), lithographic edition (Shanghai: Chung-kuo t'u-shu kung-ssu, 1909), 40 ts'e.

Tseng Kuo-fan 曾國藩, Tseng Wen-cheng-kung shu-cha 曾文正公書札 (Official correspondence of Tseng Kuo-fan), 33 chüan, in Tseng Wen-cheng-kung ch'üan-chi.

Tseng Kuo-fan 曾國藩, Tseng Wen-cheng-kung tsou-kao 曾文正公奏稿 (Draft memorials of Tseng Kuo-fan), 36 chüan, in Tseng Wen-cheng-kung ch'üan-chi.

Tseng Kuo-fan 曾國藩, Tseng Wen-cheng-kung ta-shih-chi 曾文正公大事記 (Important events in the career of Tseng Kuo-fan), in Tseng Wen-cheng-kung ch'üan-chi.

Tseng Kuo-fan, see also Wang Ting-an.

Tseng Po 曾樸 (Pen-name: Tung-ya ping-fu 東亞病夫), Nieh-hai hua 孽海花 (Beauties in the troublesome sea; Shanghai: Chen-mei-shan shu-tien, 1931), 222 pp.

Tseng Shih-o 曾士莪, "Ou-yang Pai-yuan t'an Cheng Wen-cheng-kung i-shih" 歐陽伯元談曾文正公軼事 (Ou-yang Pai-yuan's reminiscences of Tseng Kuo-fan), Kuo-wen chou-pao, 12.30: 1-3 (1935).

Tseng Shih-o 曾士莪, "Shu Weng-Li hsiang-ch'ing shih" 書翁李相傾事 (A note on the struggle between Weng T'ung-ho and Li Hung-chang), Kuo-wen chou-pao, 12.27: 1-2 (July 1935).

Tseng Wen-cheng-kung, see Tseng Kuo-fan.

Tseng Yu-hao 曾友豪, Modern Chinese Legal and Political Philosophy (Shanghai: Commercial Press, 1930), 320 pp.

Tsiang, T. F., "Bismarck and the introduction of international law into China," CSPSR, 15: 98-101 (1931).

Tsiang, T. F., "Difficulties of Reconstruction after the Treaty of Nanking," CSPSR, 16.2: 319-327 (1932-33).

Tsiang, T. F., "Sino-Japanese Diplomatic Relations, 1870-1890," CSPSR, 17.1: 107-169 (1933).

Tsiang (Chiang) Ting-fu 蔣廷黻, Chin-tai Chung-kuo wai-chiao-shih tzu-liao chi-yao 近代中國外交史資料輯要 (Selected documents on modern Chinese diplomatic history), 2 vols. (Shanghai: Commercial Press, 1931 and 1934).

Tso-chuan, see Ch'un-ch'iu Tso-chüan cheng-i.

Tso Shun-sheng 左舜生, "Chung-Jih wai-chiao-shih shang chih Li Hung-chang" 中日外交史上之李鴻章 (Li Hung-chang's position in the history of Sino-Japanese relations), Wai-chiao p'ing-lun 外交評論, 6.3: 23-47 (1936).

Tso Tsung-t'ang 左宗棠, Tso Wen-hsiang-kung ch'üan-chi 左文襄公全集 (Complete works of Tso Tsung-t'ang), including Tso Wen-hsiang-kung nien-p'u 左文襄公年譜, 100 chüan, 96 ts'e (Changsha, 1889).

Tso Tsung-t'ang 左宗棠, Tso Wen-hsiang-kung tsou-kao 左文襄公奏稿 (The memorials of Tso Tsung-t'ang), in Tso Wen-hsiang-kung ch'üan-chi, ts'e 6-7.

Tso Tsung-t'ang 左宗棠, Tso Wen-hsiang-kung shu-tu 左文襄公書牘 (The letters of Tso Tsung-t'ang), in Tso Wen-hsiang-kung ch'üan-chi, ts'e 71-96.

Tso Tsung-t'ang 左宗棠, et al., Ch'uan-cheng tsou-i hui-pien 船政奏議彙編 (Collection of memorials on marine policy), 16 ts'e (1882).

Tsou Lu 鄒魯, Chung-kuo Kuo-min-tang shih-kao 中國國民黨史稿 (Draft history of the National People's Party of China), 2 vols. (Shanghai: Min-chih shu-chü, 1929).

Tsui-chin chih wu-shih-nien, see Shen-pao-kuan.

Tsui-chin san-shih-wu-nien chih Chung-kuo chiao-yü, see Chuang Yü and Ho Sheng-nai, ed.

Tsui Shu-ch'in 崔書琴, "The Influence of the Canton-Moscow Entente upon Sun Yat-sen's Revolutionary Tactics," CSPSR, 20.1: 101-139 (April, 1936). Also Tsui's doctoral dissertation with a similar title, Department of Government, Harvard University.

Tung-fang tsa-chih 東方雜誌 (Eastern Miscellany), published in Shanghai, beginning 1904, semi-monthly, or monthly.

Tung Hsün 董恂, Huan-tu-wo-shu shih lao-jen nien-p'u 還讀我書室老人年譜 (Chronological biography of Tung Hsun), 2 chüan (Peking, 1892).

T'ung-wen kuan t'i-ming lu 同文館題名錄 (English title: The Calendar of the Tungwen College), first issue, published by authority (Peking, 1879).

Tung-ya ping-fu, see Tseng Po.

Ueda Toshio 植田捷雄, "Ahen sensō to Shimmatsu kammin no shoshō" 阿片戰爭と清末官民の諸相 ("The Actual Attitude of the Chinese Mandarins and common people towards the Opium War"), Kokusaihō gaikō zasshi 國際外交雜誌 50.3: 235-271 (July 1951).

Varg, Paul A., "William W. Rockhill's Influence on the Boxers' Negotiations," Pacific Historical Review, XVIII.3: 369-380 (August 1949).

Wada Sei 和田清, "Ri Kō-shō to sono jidai" 李鴻章とその時代 (Li Hung-chang and his times), pp. 139-155 in his Tōashi ronsō 東亞史論藪 (Essays in East Asian history; Tōkyō: Seikatsu 生活, 1942), 579 pp.

Waley, Arthur, The Analects of Confucius, translated and annotated (London: Allen and Unwin, 1938), 268 pp.

Wang Ch'in-yü 王勤堉, "Pai-nien-lai Chung-kuo t'ieh-lu shih-yeh" 百年來中國鐵路事業 (Chinese railroads during the past hundred years), Hsueh-lin, 2.40: 69-103 (December 1940).

Wang Chü-ch'ang, see Yen Fu, Yen Chi-tao nien-p'u.

Wang Ch'uan-shan, see Wang Fu-chih.

Wang Feng-yuan 王豐園, Chung-kuo hsin-wen-hsueh yun-tung shu-p'ing 中國新文學運動述評 (Narration of and comments on the new literature movement in China; Peiping: Hsin-hsin hsueh-she, 1935), 188 pp.

Wang Fu-chih 王夫之, Wang Ch'uan-shan i-shu 王船山遺書 (Writings of Wang Ch'uan-shan), 130 ts'e (published by Tseng Kuo-fan, 1865).

Wang Fu-chih 王夫之, Shih kuang-chuan 詩廣傳 (Extended commentaries on the Odes), in Wang Ch'uan-shan i-shu, ts'e 15.

Wang Fu-chih 王夫之, Huang-shu 黃書, in Wang Ch'uan-shan i-shu, ts'e 105.

Wang Fu-chih 王夫之, O Meng 噩夢, in Wang Ch'uan-shan i-shu, ts'e 105.

Wang Fu-chih 王夫之, Ssu-wen-lu wai-pien 思問錄外編, in Wang Ch'uan-shan i-shu, ts'e 105.

Wang Fu-chih 王夫之, Tu T'ung-chien lun 讀通鑑論 (Comments on reading [Ssu-ma Kuang's] Tzu-chih t'ung-chien), 30 + 1 chüan (movable type edition, Commercial Press, undated).

Wang Fu-chih, see Wang Yung-hsiang.

Wang Hsi-ch'i 王錫祺, ed., Hsiao-fang-hu-chai yü-ti ts'ung-ch'ao 小方壺齋輿地叢鈔 (Collection of geographical works from Hsiao-fang-hu Studio), preface dated 1877, Shanghai, Chu-I-t'ang 著易堂 edition, originally 1200 titles, 64 ts'e; Pu-pien 補編 (Supplement I), 58 titles, 4 ts'e; Tsai pu-pien 再補編 (Supplement II), 180 titles, 16 ts'e.

Wang Hsien-ch'ien 王先謙, Tung-hua ch'üan-lu 東華全錄, including Hsü-lu T'ung-chih, 252 ts'e, (Peking: Ch'in-wen shu-chü, 1887).

Wang Hsien-ch'ien 王先謙, Hsü-shou-t'ang shu-cha 虛受堂書札 (Collection of letters of Wang Hsien-ch'ien), 1907 edition.

Wang Hsin-chung 王信忠, "Fu-chou ch'uan-ch'ang chih yen-ko" 福州船廠之沿革 (The Development of the Foochow shipyard), Ch'ing-hua hsueh-pao, 8.1: 1-57 (December 1932). Pages of this journal not consecutively numbered.

Wang Kuang 王洸, Chung-kuo hang-yeh lun 中國航業論 (On the Chinese shipping business), Chiao-t'ung tsa-chih she ts'ung-shu 交通雜誌社叢書 (Communications Magazine series), no. 1 (Nanking: published by the Chiao-t'ung tsa-chih she, 1934), 143 pp.

Wang Shen-jan 王森然, Chin-tai erh-shih-chia p'ing-chuan 近代二十家評傳 (Critical biographies of twenty famous persons of recent times; Peiping, 1934), 406 pp.

Wang Shou-ch'ien 王守謙, "Chung-kuo chi-ch'i p an chu-tsao chih-ch'ien yü yin-yuan chih ch'i-yuan" 中國機器版鑄造制錢與銀元之起源 (The beginning of machine minting of coins and silver dollars in China), Ch'üan-pi 泉幣, no. 20.

Wang T'ao 王韜, Fu-sang yu-chi 扶桑遊記 (A record of travels in Japan), 3 chüan (printed in Japan, 1880).

Wang T'ao 王韜, T'ao-yuan wen-lu wai-pien 韜園文錄外編 (Supplement to T'ao-yuan wen-lu), 12 chüan (Hong Kong, 1882).

Wang T'ao 王韜, "Chi Ying-kuo cheng-chih" 紀英國政治 (A note on the British government), in T'ao-yuan wen-lu wai-pien.

Wang T'ao 王韜, "Chih-chung" 治中 (On domestic administration), in T'ao-yuan wen-lu wai-pien.

Wang T'ao 王韜, "Ch'u e-wai ch'üan-li" 除額外權利 (On the abolition of extraterritoriality), in T'ao-yuan wen-lu wai-pien.

Wang T'ao 王韜, "Man-yu sui-lu" 漫遊隨錄 (Notes of travels), in T'ao-yuan wen-lu wai-pien.

Wang T'ao 王韜, "Pien-fa" 變法 (On Reform), in T'ao-yuan wen-lu wai-pien.

Wang T'ao 王韜, "Shang tang-lu lun shih-wu shu" 上當路論時務書 (A letter submitted to the authorities discussing current affairs), in T'ao-yuan wen-lu wai-pien.

Wang T'ao 王韜, "Yuan-hsueh" 原學 in T'ao-yuan wen-lu wai-pien.

Wang T'ao 王韜, T'ao-yuan ch'ih-tu 韜園尺牘 (Letters of Wang T'ao), 12 chüan (printed 1886).

Wang T'ao 王韜, Hsi-hsueh chi-ts'un 西學輯存 (Collection of works on Western knowledge), 2 ts'e (Sung-yin-lu 淞隱廬 edition, 1889-90).

Wang Te-chao 王德昭, "T'ung-chih hsin-cheng k'ao" 同治新政考 (A study of the new administration of the T'ung-chih period), Wen-shih tsa-chih 文史雜誌, 1.4, 5: 21-38, 33-46 (January 1941).

Wang Te-liang 王德亮, Tseng Kuo-fan chih min-tsu ssu-hsiang 曾國藩之民族思想 (Tseng Kuo-fan's ideas on min-tsu [nationalism]; Shanghai: Commercial Press, 1946), 48 pp.

Wang Ting-an 王定安, Ch'iu-ch'ueh-chai ti-tzu chi 求闕齋弟子記 (A sketch of Tseng Kuo-fan by his disciple from the Ch'iu-ch'ueh-chai [study]), 32 chüan (1876).

Wang Ting-an 王定安, Tseng Wen-cheng-kung shih-lueh 曾文正公事畧 (A brief account of Tseng Kuo-fan), 2 ts'e (1875).

Wang Tsao-shih 王造時 , "Chung-Hsi chieh-ch'u-hou she-hui-shang ti pien-hua" 中西接觸後社會上的變化 (Social changes after the contact between China and the West), Tung-fang tsa-chih, 31.2: 31-40 (1934).

Wang Yen-wei 王彥威 , comp., Ch'ing-chi wai-chiao shih-liao 清季外交史料 (Historical materials on late Ch'ing diplomacy), 112 ts'e (Peking: movable-type edition, 1932-1935).

Wang Yun-sheng 王芸生 , "Chung-E mi-yueh pien-wei" 中俄密約辨偽 (Discrimination between [truth and] falsehood in the Sino-Russian secret pacts), Kuo-wen chou-pao, 9.28: 1-4 (July 1932).

Wang Yun-sheng 王芸生 , comp., Liu-shih-nien-lai Chung-kuo yü Jih-pen 六十年來中國與日本 (China and Japan during the last sixty years), 6 vols. (Tientsin: published by Ta-kung-pao 大公報 , 1932-1933).

Wang Yung 王庸 , Chung-kuo ti-li-hsueh shih 中國地理學史 (History of Chinese geography; Changsha: Commercial Press, 1938), 262 pp.

Wang Yung-hsiang 王永祥 , Ch'uan-shan hsueh-p'u 船山學譜 (A chronological account of the scholarship of Wang Fu-chih), 6 chüan (Peiping: movable-type edition by Sui-ya-chai 邃雅齋 , 1934).

Ward, J. S. M., and Sterling, W. G., The Hung Society or the Society of Heaven and Earth, 3 vols. (London, 1926), 180 + 196 + 148 pp. See also Pelliot.

Webster, James B., Christian Education and the National Consciousness in China (New York, 1923), 323 pp.

Wegneuer, Dr. Georg, "Der Gouverneur von Shantung," Deutsche Kolonialzeitung, 27: 249-250 (June 1901).

Wei Hsi-yü 韋息予 , Li Hung-chang 李鴻章 (Shanghai: Chunghua Book Company, 1931), 95 pp.

Wei Ying-ch'i, see Lin Tse-hsü, Lin Wen-chung-kung nien-p'u.

Wei Yuan 魏源, Hai-kuo t'u-chih 海國圖志 (An illustrated gazetteer of the maritime countries), first block-print edition of 50 chüan (1844, preface by Wei Yuan dated 1842). Later editions noted in Chapter III.

Wei Yuan 魏源, Sheng-wu chi 聖武記 (Record of imperial military exploits), 12 ts'e (1842); (reprinted 1927 and 1930), 14 chüan in 6 ts'e.

Wei Yün-kung 魏允恭 , Chiang-nan chih-tsao-chü chi 江南製造局記 (An account of the Kiang-nan Arsenal), 10 chüan (Shanghai, 1905).

Wen-che chi-k'an 文哲季刊 (Quarterly Journal of Liberal Arts), Wuhan University, Wuchang, beginning 1930, quarterly.

(Wen-hsiang 文祥), Wen Wen-chung-kung shih-lueh 文文忠公事略 (A brief account of Wen-hsiang), 4 chüan (printed, 1882).

Wen-hsien ts'ung-pien 文獻叢編 (Miscellaneous publication of the government archives), Peiping, Palace Museum, beginning 1930, monthly.

Wen T'ing-ching 溫廷敬 , "Huang Tsun-hsien chuan" 黃遵憲傳 (A biography of Huang Tsun-hsien), Kuo-feng, 5. 8-9: 3-7 (November 1934).

Wen Yuan-ning, "Ku Hung-ming," T'ien-hsia monthly, 4.4: 386-398 (April 1937).

Weng Wen-hao 翁文灝 , "Wu-shih-nien-lai chih ching-chi chien-she" 五十年來之經濟建設 (Economic reconstruction during the last 50 years), in Wu-shih-nien-lai ti Chung-kuo 五十年來 的中國 (China in the last 50 years), compiled by P'an Kung-chan 潘公展 (Chungking: published by Sheng-li shu-tien, 1944).

Wieger, Léon, ed. and tr., Chine Moderne, 10 vols. (Hsien-hsien, 1922-27).

Wilbur, C. Martin, ed., Chinese Sources on the History of the Chinese Communist Movement, an annotated bibliography of materials in the East Asiatic Library of Columbia University (reproduced for private distribution by the East Asia Institute, Columbia University, 1950), 55 pp.

Wilhelm, Hellmut, The attitude of the early Ch'ing scholars toward the Manchus (mimeographed for private distribution, Far Eastern Institute, University of Washington, 1949).

Wilhelm, Hellmut, "The background of Tseng Kuo-fan's ideology," Asiatische Studien, 3. 3-4: 90-100 (1949).

Wilhelm, Hellmut, "The problem of within and without, a Confucian attempt in syncretism," Journal of the History of Ideas, 12.1: 48-60 (January 1951).

Wilson, James Harrison, China, Travels and Investigations in the "Middle Kingdom," third edition revised (New York, 1901), 429 pp.

Wen Kung-chih 文公直 , Tsui-chin san-shih-nien Chung-kuo chün-shih shih 最近三十年中國軍 事史 (History of Chinese military affairs in the last thirty years), 2 vols. (Shanghai: T'ai-p'ing-yang shu-tien, 1930).

Wo-jen 倭仁 , Wo Wen-tuan-kung i-shu 倭文端公遺書 (Collected writings of Wo-jen), 11 chüan, 8 ts'e (block-print edition, 1882).

Wong, K. C. and Wu, L. T., History of Chinese Medicine (Tientsin: Tientsin Press, 1932), 706 pp.

Woodbridge, Samuel I., China's Only Hope, An Appeal by Her Greatest Viceroy, Chang Chih-tung (New York, 1900), 151 pp.

Wright, Authur F., "Fu I and the Rejection of Buddhism," in "Chinese Reactions to Imported Ideas, a Symposium," Journal of the History of Ideas, 12.1: 33-47 (January 1951).

Wright, Mary C., "The T'ung-chih Restoration" (Ph.D. dissertation in History, Radcliffe College, 1951).

Wright, S. F., Hart and the Chinese Customs (Belfast: published for the Queen's University by W. Mullan, 1950), 949 pp.

Wu, Chao Kwang, The International Aspect of the Missionary Movement in China (Baltimore: Johns Hopkins Press, 1930), 285 pp.

Wu Ch'eng-chang 吳成章 , Wai-chiao-pu yen-ko chi-lueh 外交部沿革紀略 (A brief account of the reforms in the Wai-chiao-pu), 1 ts'e (Peking: Wai-chiao-pu Press, 1913).

Wu Ch'i-ch'ang 吳其昌 , Liang Ch'i-ch'ao 梁啟超 (Liang Ch'i-ch'ao; Chungking: Sheng-li ch'u-pan-she, 1944), 127 pp.

Wu Ch'i-yuan 伍啟元 , Chung-kuo hsin-wen-hua yun-tung kai-kuan 中國新文化運動概觀 (A general review of China's new culture movement; Shanghai: Hsien-tai shu-chü, 1934), 180 pp.

Wu Ching-heng 吳敬恆 , Wu Chih-hui hsien-sheng wen-ts'un 吳稚暉先生文存 (Collected essays of Wu Chih-hui), 2 vols. (Shanghai: I-hsueh shu-chü, 1925).

Wu Hsuan-i 吳宣易 , "Ching-shih T'ung-wen kuan lueh-shih" 京師同文館略史 (An historical sketch of the T'ung-wen Kuan at Peking), Tu-shu yueh-k'an 讀書月刊 , 2.4: 1-15 (1933).

Wu, James T. K., "The Impact of the Taiping Rebellion upon the Manchu Fiscal System," <u>Pacific Historical Review</u> 19: 265-75 (August 1950).

Wu Ju-lun 吳汝綸, <u>T'ung-ch'eng Wu hsien-sheng ch'üan-shu</u> 桐城吳先生全書 (Complete works of Mr. Wu of T'ung-ch'eng), 20 <u>ts'e</u> (1904).

Wu Ju-lun 吳汝綸, <u>T'ung-ch'eng Wu hsien-sheng jih-chi</u> 桐城吳先生日記 (The diary of Wu Ju-lun), 16 <u>chüan</u>, 10 <u>ts'e</u> (Pao-ting : Lien-ch'ih shu-she, 1928).

Wu Pao-chang 吳保璋, "Li Wen-chung-kung pai-shih-chou-nien chi-nien kan-yen" 李文忠公百十週年紀念感言 (A word in commemoration of Li Hung-chang's 110th birthday), <u>Hsueh-feng</u>, 4.7: 1-4 (1934).

Wu Po 武波 (Fan Wen-lan 范文瀾), <u>Chung-kuo chin-tai shih</u> 中國近代史 (A history of modern China; Shanghai: Tu-shu ch'u-pan-she, 1947), 418 pp.

Wu Sheng-te 吳盛德 and Ch'en Tseng-hui 陳增輝, <u>Chiao-an shih-liao pien-mu</u> 教案史料編目 (Catalogue of historical materials on missionary cases; Peiping: Yenching School of Religion Series, no. 5, 1941), 227 pp.

Wu-shih-nien-lai ti Chung-kuo, see P'an Kung-chan.

Wu T'ing-fang 伍廷芳, <u>Min-kuo t'u-chih ch'u-i</u> 民國圖治芻議 (Opinions regarding the advancement of good government under the Republic; Shanghai: published by the author, 1915), 107 pp.

Wu Tse 吳澤, <u>K'ang Yu-wei yü Liang Ch'i-ch'ao</u> 康有為與梁啟超 (K'ang Yu-wei and Liang Ch'i-ch'ao; Shanghai, 1948), 202 pp.

Wu Tse 吳澤, "Lun pien-fa chih ching-shen" 論變法之精神 (On the spirit of reform), <u>Tung-fang tsa-chih</u>, 7: 142-144 (1904).

Wu Tse 吳澤, "Pao-huang-tang yü K'ang-Liang lu-hsien" 保皇黨與康梁路線 (The Royalist Party and the policy of K'ang and Liang), <u>Chung-kuo chien-she,</u> 7.1: 44-47 (October 1948).

Wu Tse 吳澤, "Wu-hsü cheng-pien yü hsin-chiu tang-cheng" 戊戌政變與新舊黨爭 (The coup d'état of 1898 and the struggle between the old and new factions), <u>Chung-kuo chien-she</u> 6.6: 42-45 (September 1948).

Wu Yü-kan 武堉幹, "Liu-shih-nien Chung-kuo shang-yeh chih fa-chan" 六十年中國商業之發展 (The development of Chinese commerce in the past 60 years), <u>Shen-pao yueh-k'an</u> 申報月刊, 1.1: 19-34 (July 1932).

Wylie, Alexander, <u>Memorials of Protestant Missionaries to the Chinese: giving a list of their publications, and obituary notices of the deceased</u> (Shanghai, 1867), 331 pp.

Yamamoto Sumiko 山本澄子, "Giwadan no seikaku ni tsuite" 義和拳の性格に就いて (On the social character of the Boxer Rebellion), <u>Shikan</u> 史觀 ("The Historical Review, edited by Historical Society of Waseda University"), no. 33: 45-61 (April 1950).

Yang Ch'üan 楊銓, "Wu-shih-nien-lai Chung-kuo chih kung-yeh" 五十年來中國之工業 (China's industrial enterprise during the past 50 years), in <u>Tsui-chin chih wu-shih-nien</u>, pp. 1-15.

Yang Hung-lieh 楊鴻烈, "Chi Kuo Sung-tao ch'u-shih Ying-Fa" 記郭松燾出使英法 (An account of Kuo Sung-tao's mission to England and France), <u>Ku-chin</u>, nos. 11-12 (1942 ? page numbers unavailable).

Yang Hung-lieh 楊鴻烈, "Chung-kuo she-chih chu-I shih-kuan ti ching-kuo" 中國設置駐義使館的經過 (History of the establishment of the Chinese legation in Italy), <u>Ku-chin</u>, no. 25: 11-15 (June 1943), and no. 26: 19-23 (July 1943).

Yang Hung-lieh 楊鴻烈, "Chung-kuo chu-wai shih-kuan chih-tu ti chien-t'ao" 中國駐外使館制度的檢討 (An examination of the system of Chinese diplomatic missions abroad), Tung-fang wen-hua 東方文化, 21 (1944 ?).

Yang Kuang-hsien 楊光先, Pu-te-i 不得已 (I could not keep silent), photolithographic edition, 2 ts'e (1929). See also the Sheng-ch'ao p'o-hsieh-chi Japanese edition of 1855.

Yang K'un 楊堃, "Chung-kuo tsui-chin san-shih-nien chih ch'u-pan chieh: she-hui-hsüeh chih pu" 中國最近三十年之出版界,社會學之部 (Chinese publications during the past thirty years: books on sociology), Kuo-li hua-pei pien-i-kuan kuan-k'an, 國立華北編輯館館刊, 2.7: 1-19 (July, 1944).

Yang, Lien-sheng, Money and Credit in China, A Short History (Cambridge: Harvard University Press, 1952), 143 pp.

Yang, Lien-sheng, Topics in Chinese History, Harvard-Yenching Institute Studies, vol. 4 (Cambridge: Harvard University Press, 1950), 57 pp.

Yang Lu 楊魯, K'ai-luan-k'uang li-shih chi shou-kuei kuo-yu wen-t'i 開灤礦歷史及收歸國有問題 (The history of the Kailan Mine and the question of its restoration to Chinese national ownership; Tientsin: published by the author, 1932), 210 pp.

Yang Ping-nan 楊炳南, Hai-lu 海錄 (Maritime record), in Hsiao-fang-hu-chai yü-ti ts'ung-ch'ao, ts'e 55.

Yang Ta-chin 楊大金, Hsien-tai Chung-kuo shih-yeh chih 現代中國實業誌 (Modern Chinese industry), revised edition, 2 vols. (Shanghai: Commercial Press, 1938).

Yang Ta-shu 楊大樹, "Tseng Kuo-fan ti ssu-hsiang" 曾國藩的思想 (Tseng Kuo-fan's ideas), Hsin wen-hua yüeh-k'an 新文化月刊, nos. 3-4, 5 (not consulted).

Yang Wei-yü and P'an Kung-chao 楊衛玉,潘公昭, "K'ang-hsi-ti yü Hsi-yang wen-hua" 康熙帝與西洋文化 (Emperor K'ang-hsi and Western culture), Tu-shu t'ung-hsin 讀書通訊, no. 121: 8-11 (November 1946).

Yang Yung-kuo 楊榮國, "Li Shou-ch'ang hsien-sheng ti ssu-hsiang" 李守常先生的思想 (Li Shou-ch'ang's ideas), Tu-shu yü ch'u-pan 讀書與出版, 2.1: 4-7 (1947).

Yano Jin'ichi 矢野仁一, Nisshin ekigo Shina gaikō shi 日清役後支那外交史 ("A History of the Post-bellum Diplomacy of China after the Sino-Japanese War"), Memoirs, vol. 9 (Kyōto: Tōhō bunka gakuin, Kyōto kenkyūsho [The Academy of Oriental Culture, Kyōto Institute], 1937), 709 pp.; index and bibliography, 21 pp.; English summary, 17 pp.

Yano Jin'ichi 矢野仁一, Shinchō matsushi kenkyū 清朝末史研究 (Researches in late-Ch'ing history; Ōsaka: Daiwa shoin, 1944), 342 pp.

Yano Jin'ichi 矢野仁一, "Bojutsu no hempo oyobi seihen" 戊戌の變法及び政變 (The 1898 reforms and coup d'état), Shirin 史林, 8.1: 54-67 (1923); 8.2: 30-44; and 8.3: 81-100.

Yao Pao-yü 姚寶猷, "Chi-tu-chiao chiao-shih shu-ju Hsi-yang wen-hua k'ao" 基督教教士輸入西洋文化攷 (The introduction of Western civilization into China: a study of the activities of the Christian missionaries), Shih-hsüeh chuan-k'an 史學專刊, 1.2: 1-66 (February 1936).

Yazawa Toshihiko 矢澤利彦, Chūgoku to Seiyō bunka 中國と西洋文化 (China and Western culture; Tōkyō: Nakamura shoten, 1947), 199 pp.

Yeh Ch'ing 葉青, Hu Shih p'i-p'an 胡適批判 (Critique of Hu Shih), "The Critiques Series B," edited by Erh-shih shih-chi she 二十世紀社 (The Twentieth Century ; Shanghai: Hsin-k'en shu-tien, 1933), 28 + 1148 pp.

Yeh Te-hui 葉德輝 , Chüeh-mi yao-lu 覺迷要錄 (Essential writings for awakening the misled), 4 chüan, special series, published by Yeh Te-hui (1905).

Yen Chung-p'ing 嚴中平 , Chung-kuo mien-yeh chih fa-chan 中國棉業之發展 (The development of the Chinese cotton industry), Academia Sinica Series (Chungking: Commercial Press, 1943), 305 pp.

Yen Fu, The Story of a Chinese Oxford Movement (1910). Complete information not available.

Yen Fu 嚴復, Yen Chi-tao shih-wen ch'ao 嚴幾道詩文鈔 (Collected works of Yen Fu), 6 ts'e (Shanghai: Kuo-hua shu-chü, 1922).

Yen Fu 嚴復 , "Yen Chi-tao yü Hsiung Shun-ju shu-cha chieh-ch'ao" 嚴幾道與熊純如書札節鈔 (Excerpts from the correspondence between Yen Chi-tao and Hsiung Shun-ju), Hsueh-heng 學衡, no. 18 (1923).

Yen Fu 嚴復 , letters no. 58-59 in Hsueh-heng, no. 18: 6-7 (1923).

(Yen Fu 嚴復), Yen Chi-tao nien-p'u 嚴幾道年譜 (A chronological biography of Yen Fu), by Wang Chü-ch'ang 王蘧常 (Shanghai: Commercial Press, 1936), 138 pp. See also Lin Yao-hua.

Yin-hang nien-chien, see Ch'üan-kuo yin-hang nien-chien.

Yü Ch'ang-ho 余長河 , "Kuo Sung-tao yü Chung-kuo wai-chiao" 郭嵩燾與中國外交 (Kuo Sung-tao and Chinese diplomacy), I-ching, no. 31: 21-24 (1937).

Yü Yueh 俞樾 , Pin-meng chi 賓萌集 , in Ch'un-tsai-t'ang ch'üan-shu 春在堂全書 (Complete works of Yü Yueh), ts'e 61 (1899).

Yü Yueh 俞樾 , "San ta-yu lun" 三大憂論 (On the three great anxieties), in Pin-meng-chi, chüan 6.

Yuan Chen-ying 袁振英 , "Ku Hung-ming hsien-sheng ti ssu-hsiang" 辜鴻銘先生的思想 (Ku Hung-ming's ideas), Jen-chien shih, no. 34: 3-6 (August 1935).

Yuan Shih-k'ai 袁世凱 , Hsin-chien lu-chün ping-lueh lu-ts'un 新建陸軍兵略錄存 (A collection of available military plans for the new army), 6 chüan, 6 ts'e (movable-type edition of 1898).

Yuan Tao-feng, "Li Hung-chang and the Sino-Japanese War," T'ien Hsia Monthly, 3.1: 9-17 (1936).

Yuan Tsu-chih 袁祖志 , She-yang kuan-chien 涉洋管見 (Personal point of view after travelling to foreign countries), in Hsiao-fang-hu-chai yü-ti ts'ung-ch'ao, ts'e 60.

Yung Shang Him (Jung Shang-ch'ien 容尚謙), "The Chinese Educational Mission and Its Influence," T'ien Hsia Monthly, 9.3: 225-256 (October 1939).

Yung Wing, My Life in China and America (New York, 1909), 286 pp.

GLOSSARY

This single alphabetic list by Wade-Giles romanization (omitting most diacritical marks) provides Chinese characters for personal names, for technical terms or quoted phrases in the text and notes, and for book and periodical titles which do not occur in the Bibliography.

Ai-li-shih 埃利士 (Irish)

An Ch'ung-ken 安重根

An-fu 安福

cha-p'ao 炸炮

Chang Chün-mai 張君勱

Chang Hsing-yen 章行嚴
  (Chang Shih-chao 章士釗)

Chang Hsün 張勳

chang-san-shih 張三世

Chang Tso-lin 張作霖

Chang Tung-sun 張東蓀

Ch'ang-shih chi 嘗試集

ch'ang-yueh 廠約

Chao Shu-ch'iao 趙舒翹

ch'en 辰

Ch'en Chi-ju 陳繼儒

Ch'en Chiung-ming 陳炯明

Ch'en Lan-pin 陳蘭彬

Ch'en Li-fu 陳立夫

Ch'en Pao-chen 陳寶箴

Ch'en Yuan-chi 陳遠濟

Ch'eng 程

Ch'eng Hsueh-ch'i 程學啟

Chi-er-hang-a 吉爾杭阿

ch'i 氣

Ch'i 齊

ch'i 器

Ch'i-hsiu 啟秀

Ch'i-shan 琦善

Chia-ch'ing 嘉慶

Chia I 賈誼

Chia-yin tsa-chih 甲寅雜誌

Chiang Chung-yuan 江忠源

Chiang I-li 蔣益澧

Chiang-nan chih-tsao tsung-chu 江南製造總局

Ch'iang-hsueh hui 強學會

Ch'iang-kuo chih hui 強國之會

Chiao-shih-kuan 校士館

chiao-tzu 交子

chiao-yü chiu-kuo 教育救國

Chieh 桀

Ch'ien Cheng 錢徵

Ch'ien-ch'ing 乾清

ch'ien-chuang 錢莊

Ch'ien Hsuan-t'ung 錢玄同

Ch'ien-lung 乾隆

chih 旨

Chih-kang 志剛

Ch'ih-yu 蚩尤

Chin 金

Chin Ai-li 陳愛麗

Chin Kao-tsu, see Shih Ching-t'ang

chin-shih 進士

Chin-te-hui 進德會

chin-wen chia 今文家

ching-chi t'e-k'o 經濟特科

ching-shih chih-yung 經世致用

Ch'ing-i pao 清議報

Chiu-chou 九州

Chiu Kaiming 裘開明

Chiu-shih chieh-yao 救世揭要

Chou 紂

Chou Fu 周馥

Chou-pi suan-ching 周髀算經

Chou Tzu-yü 周子愚

ch'ou 丑

ch'ou 籌

Ch'ou-an-hui 籌安會

ch'ou-suan 籌算

Chu Hsi 朱熹

Chu Hung-teng 朱紅燈

chü-jen 舉人

Ch'u 楚

Ch'ü Yuan 屈原

Ch'uan-ching-lou 傳經樓

ch'üan-min cheng-chih 全民政治

ch'üan-p'an hsi-hua 全盤西化

Chuang Yü 莊嶽

chuang-yuan 狀元

chün-chu kuo 君主國

chün kuo-min chiao-yü 君國民教育

chün-min kung-chu kuo 君民共主國

chung, hsin, tu, ching 忠, 信, 篤, 敬

Chung-hua 中華

Chung-hsueh wei t'i, Hsi-hsueh wei yung
中學為體, 西學為用

Chung-hua ko-ming-tang 中華革命黨

Chung-kuo t'ung-shang yin-hang 中國通商銀行

(China Commercial Bank)

Chung-t'ao, see Wang T'ao

Ch'ung-hou 崇厚

fa-tsu 法祖

Fang Chao-ying 房兆楹

Fang I-chih 方以智

Fang-lueh-kuan 方略館

Fang Pao 方苞

Feng Chün-kuang 馮焌光

Feng Kuo-chang 馮國璋

feng-shui 風水

Feng Ying-ching 馮應京

Fo-lang-chi 佛郎機
 ("Franks," the Portuguese)

Fo-lang-hsi 佛郎西 (France)

fu 賦

fu-Ch'ing mieh-yang 扶清滅洋

Fu K'uei 傅夔

fu-kung-sheng 附貢生

fu-ping 府兵

Fu Yueh-fen 傅嶽芬

Hai-chün Ya-men 海軍衙門

Han-cho 寒浞

Ho Kuo-tsung 何國宗

Ho-lan 荷蘭 (Holland)

hou-ju 後儒

Hsi-li 息力 (Singapore)

Hsi T'ai-hou, see Tz'u-hsi

Hsi-yang 西洋

Hsi-yang jen 西洋人

Hsi-yü 西域

Hsia 夏

Hsia Tseng-yu 夏曾佑

Hsiang-chün 湘軍

Hsiang-pao 湘報

Hsiang-tao 嚮導

Hsiao-chen, see T'zu-an

Hsiao-ch'in, see Tz'u-hsi

Hsiao-wen 孝文

hsien 縣

hsien-ju 先儒

Hsien-feng 咸豐

hsien-shih 先師

hsin 心

Hsin-chiao-yü 新教育

Hsin-chien lu-chün 新建陸軍

hsin-min 新民

Hsin min-chu chu-i 新民主主義

Hsin-min chu-i 新民主義

Hsing-Chung-hui 興中會

Hsiung-nu 匈奴

Hsü Ching-ch'eng 許景澄

Hsü Chün-ch'ing (Hsü Yu-jen) 徐君青

Hsü Kuang-ch'i 徐光啟 (Paul Hsu)

Hsü Shih-ch'ang 徐世昌

Hsü Shou 徐壽

Hsü T'ung 徐桐

hsü-wu 虛無

Hsü Yu 許由

Hsuan-wu (-men) 宣武門

Hsuan-yeh 玄曄

Hsueh-chi 學記

Hsueh Huan 薛煥

Hsün-huan jih-pao 循環日報

hsün-lien yuan 訓練員

Hu Kuang-yung 胡光墉

Hu-men 虎門

Hu-pu 戶部

Hu Yü-fen 胡燏棻

Hua-sheng-tun 華盛頓

Huai-chün 淮軍

Huang En-t'ung 黃恩彤

Huang T'ao, see Wang T'ao

Huang Tsun-hsien 黃遵憲

Huang Wan, see Wang T'ao

Hui-feng yin-hang 滙豐銀行 (Hongkong and Shanghai Banking Corporation)

Hui-ming hsueh-hui 晦明學會

hui-tzu 會子

Hung-fan 洪範

Hung-mao 紅毛

Hung-men 洪門

Hung, William 洪煨蓮

i 夷

I-hsin, see Prince Kung

I-huan, see Prince Ch'un

I I (Hou I) 夷羿

I-k'uang 奕劻

i-lu-p'ing-an 一路平安

I-pu-sheng 易卜生 (Ibsen)

I-shan 奕山

i, shu, jen 義, 恕, 仁

I-ta-li 義大利 (Italy)

Ieyasu 家康

Itō Hirobumi 伊藤博文

I-yen 易言

jen-ts'ai 人才

Jo-erh-jih 若爾日 (George I)

k'an 坎

Kang-i 剛毅

K'ang-hsi 康熙

Keng Ching-chung 耿精忠

Ko-lo-pa 噶羅巴

Ku Hung-ming 辜鴻銘
 (Ku T'ang-sheng 辜湯生)

Ku-tsung 顧琮

Ku-wei-t'ang 古微堂

kuan 關

kuan-tu shang-pan 官督商辦

Kuang-hsü 光緒

Kuei-liang 桂良

kung-hui 公會

Kung-i chü 工藝局

Kung-sun Hung 公孫弘

Kuo-feng pao 國風報

kuo-min ko-ming 國民革命

Kuo Mo-jo 郭沫若

Kuo Sung-lin 郭松林

kuo-ts'ui 國粹

Kuo-wen hui-pao 國聞彙報
 (Kuo-wen-pao)

kuo-yü 國語

Lao-tzu 老子

li 里

li 理

Li 厲

Li-chi 禮記

Li Chih-tsao 李之藻

li-hai 厲害

Li Hsiu-ch'eng 李秀成

Li Hung-tsao 李鴻藻

Li Lien-ying 李蓮英

Li-ma-tou 利瑪竇 (Matteo Ricci)

li-po-erh-t'e 里勃而特 (liberty)

Li Sheng-to 李盛鐸

Li Shih-tseng 李石曾
 (Li Yü-ying 李煜瀛)

Li-yun 禮運

Liao 遼

Lien-hsing 聯興

likin 釐金

Lin Shu 林舒
 (Lin Ch'in-nan 林琴南)

Liu Fu 劉復

Liu, K. C. 劉廣京

Liu K'un-i 劉坤一

Liu Shih-p'ei 劉師培

Liu Yung-fu 劉永福

Lo-lo 羅羅

Lo Shih-lin 羅士林

Lo Tse-nan 羅澤南

Lü-hsing 呂刑

Lü-ying 綠營

Ma Chien-chung 馬建忠

Ma-kao-wen 瑪高溫 (John MacGowan)

Ma-k'o-ssu 馬克思 (Marx)

Mao 卯

mao-tzu 毛子

Mei-chou p'ing-lun 每週評論

mei-kan chih chiao-yü 美感之教育

Mei Ku-ch'eng 梅穀成

Mei Wen-ting 梅文鼎

Meng-yang-chai 蒙養齋

Miao-tzu 苗子

min-chu 民主

min-chu chih kuo 民主之國

min-chu-kuo 民主國

min-ch'üan 民權

Min-ch'üan ch'u-pu 民權初步

Min-pao 民報

min-ping 民兵

min-sheng 民生

Min-to 民鐸

min-tsu chien-kuo 民族建國

ming 名

Mo-hai shu-yuan 墨海書院
　(Muirhead Academy)

Mo-tzu 墨子

Nagaoka Ryōnosuke 長岡良之助

Nan-hsüeh-hui 南學會

Nan-huai-jen 南懷仁 (Ferdinand Verbiest)

Nan-yang 南洋

Nien 捻

nei-luan wai-huan 內亂外患

pa-cheng 霸政

Pa-kua-chiao 八卦教

pai-hua 白話

Pai-lai-ni 白來尼 (M. de Bellonet?)

Pai-lien-chiao 白蓮教

Pao-kuo-hui 保國會

Pei-ching ta-hsueh 北京大學

Pi Yuan 畢沅

p'iao 票

p'iao-hao 票號

Pien-fa t'ung-lun 變法通論

pien-fa wei-hsin 變法維新

Pin-ch'un 斌椿

Prince Ch'un (Ch'un ch'in-wang 醇親王
　I-huan 奕環)

Prince Kung (Kung ch'in-wang 恭親王
　I-hsin 奕訢)

pu 部

P'u-an-ch'en 蒲安臣 (Anson Burlingame)

San-fan 三藩

San-ho-hui 三合會

san-kang 三綱

San-k'ou t'ung-shang ta-ch'en 三口通商大臣

San-min chu-i 三民主義

Sha-chiao 沙角

Shang, Chou 商周

Shang-hai ping-kung-ch'ang 上海兵工廠

Shang-hai chih-tsao chü 上海製造局

Shang K'o-hsi 尚可喜

Shang-ti 上帝

Shang Yang 商鞅

Shen Chia-pen 沈家本

Shen-nung 神農

Shen-pao, see Shun Pao

Shen Pao - chen 沈葆楨

Shen Pao-ching 沈保靖

shen-shang 紳商

Shen Tseng-chih 沈曾植

Shen Yin-mo 沈尹默

shih 實

shih-chieh-kuan chiao-yü 世界觀教育

Shih Ching-t'ang 石敬塘
　(Chin Kao-tsu 晉高祖)

shih-k'o 十刻

shih-li chu-i chih chiao-yü 實利主義
　　　之教育

Shih-min kung-hui 士民公會

Shih-pao 時報

shih-pien 世變

Shih-wu hsueh-t'ang 時務學堂

Shih-wu pao 時務報

Shih-yeh chi-hua 實業計劃

Shu-mi-yuan 樞密院

Shun-chih 順治

Shun Pao (Shen pao) 申報

So Kuan-wai 蘇均煒

Ssu-ma I 司馬懿

Su-ko-lan 蘇格蘭 (Scotland)

su-la 蘇拉

Su Tzu-chan 蘇子瞻

Sun Chia-ku 孫家穀

Sun, E-tu Zen 孫任以都

Sung Chiao-jen 宋敎仁

Ta-chiao 大角

Ta-Ch'ing 大清

ta-ch'üan 大權

Ta-hsi-yang 大西洋

ta-tao chih hsing yeh, t'ien-hsia wei kung
大道之行也, 天下為公

ta-tao wei kung 大道為公

ta-ts'an 大餐

Tai Chen 戴震

T'ai-chi 太極

T'ai-hsi hsin-shih lan-yao 泰西新史攬要

T'an Chung-lin 譚鍾麟

T'ang 湯

T'ang Jo-wang 湯若望
　(Adam Schall von Bell)

T'ang Shun-chih 唐順之

T'ang T'ing-shu 唐廷樞

tao 道

taotai 道臺

tao-te 道德

te-t'i chou-tao 得體周到

T'e-la-ko-erh, T'an-ti-chi 特拉格爾,
　探地記 (Doudart de Lagrée, Investigation of
　the Routes, 1865)

t'ieh-ch'ang 鐵廠

t'ieh-lu 鐵路

T'ien-chi, S.S. 恬吉

T'ien-chu 天主

T'ien-chu kuo 天主國

t'ien-hsia 天下

t'ien-hsia wei kung 天下為公

T'ien-nan-tun-sou, see Wang T'ao

T'ien-yun 天運

Ting Jih-ch'ang 丁日昌
　(Ting Yü-sheng 丁雨生)

Ting Kung-ch'en 丁拱辰

Ting Pao-chen 丁寶楨

Ting-wei-liang 丁韙良 (W. A. P. Martin)

Ting Wen-ch'eng 丁文誠

Ting-wu chün 定武軍

Ting Yü-sheng, see Ting Jih-ch'ang

Tokugawa Mitsukuni 德川光圀

Tsai-chen 載振

Ts'an-mou pen-pu 參謀本部

Ts'ao-fu 巢父

Ts'ao K'un 曹錕

Ts'ao Ts'ao 曹操

Tse-k'o-lu 則克錄

Tseng Ching 曾錚

Tseng Lien 曾廉

Tseng-tzu 曾子

Tso Ping-lung 左秉隆

Tsu Ch'ung-chih 祖沖之

Tsun Wan Yat Po, see Hsün-huan jih-pao

Tsung-heng-chia 縱橫家

Tsung-li ko-kuo shih-wu ya-men 總理各國事務衙門 (Tsungli Yamen)

Tsung-ying-wu ch'u 總營務處

Tu-li p'ing-lun 獨立評論

Tu Lien-che 杜聯喆

Tu-pan cheng-wu ch'u 督辦政務處

Tuan Ch'i-jui 段祺瑞

Tuan-fang 端方

t'uan-lien 團練

Tung Fu-hsiang 董福祥

Tung T'ai-hou, see Tz'u-an

t'ung 通

T'ung-chih 同治

T'ung-meng-hui 同盟會

t'ung-san-t'ung 通三統

t'ung-shih 通事

T'ung-wen Kuan 同文館

tzu-ch'iang 自强

Tzu-ch'iang-chün 自强軍

tzu-chu 自主

tzu-yu 自由

Tz'u-an, the Empress Dowager 慈安皇太后 (Empress Hsiao-chen 孝貞顯皇后 Tung T'ai-hou 東太后)

Tz'u-hsi, the Empress Dowager 慈禧皇太后 (Empress Hsiao-ch'in 孝欽顯皇后, Hsi T'ai-hou 西太后)

Wai-pu 外部

Wai-wu-pu 外務部

Wan-kuo kung-pao 萬國公報

Wan-li 萬歷

Wan-mu ts'ao-t'ang ts'ung-k'an 萬木草堂叢刊

Wan-yen shu 萬言書

Wang An-shih 王安石

Wang Cheng 王徵

Wang Ch'ung-hui 王寵惠

Wang K'ang-nien 汪康年

Wang K'en-t'ang 王肯堂

Wang Li-pin, see Wang T'ao

Wang Shih-chen 王士珍

wang-tao 王道

Wang T'ao 王韜 (Wang Li-pin 王利賓, Huang T'ao 黃韜, Huang Wan 黃畹, Chung-t'ao 仲弢, T'ien-nan tun-sou 天南遯叟)

Wang Yang-ming 王陽明

Wei-lieh ya-li 偉烈亞力 (Alexander Wylie)

Wei Mu-t'ing 魏睦庭

Wen-hua (tien) 文華殿

wen-kuan 文館

Wen-t'i 文悌

Wen, Wu 文,武

Weng T'ung-ho 翁同龢

wo-k'ou 倭寇

Wu 吳

Wu Ch'en 巫臣

Wu Chia-pin 吳嘉賓 (Wu Tzu-hsü 吳子序)

Wu Chih-hui 吳稚暉 (Wu Ching-heng 吳敬恒)

Wu-k'ou t'ung-shang ta-ch'en 五口通商大臣

Wu-ling 武靈

Wu-pei hsueh-t'ang 武備學堂

Wu San-kuei 吳三桂

Wu-ti 武帝

Wu Tzu-hsü, see Wu Chia-pin

Wu Tzu-teng 吳子登

Wu Yuan-ping 吳元炳

yang-hsing 養性

Yang Lien-sheng 楊聯陞

Yang T'ing-yun 楊庭筠 (Michael Yang)

yang-wu 洋務

Yao, Shun 堯,舜

Yao-tien 堯典

Yeh-lang 夜郎

Yeh Ming-ch'en 葉名琛

Yeh Te-hui 葉德輝

Yen Hsiu 嚴修

Yen Hsin-hou 嚴信厚

Yen-p'ao t'u-shuo 演礮圖說

yin 寅

yin-hao 銀號

yin, yang 陰,陽

Ying-hua shu-yuan 英華書院

Ying Kuei 英桂

Ying-kuo wang 英國王

Yo Fei 岳飛

Yu 幽

Yü, Hsia 虞夏

Yü-hsien 毓賢

Yü-lu 裕祿

Yü Shih-mei 于式枚

Yuan Ch'ang 袁昶

Yuan-ming-yuan 圓明園

Yue, Zunvair 于震寰

yueh 月

Yung-cheng 雍正

yung-hsia pien-i 用夏變夷

Yung Wing (Jung Hung) 容閎